Everly A. Kintner,
5251 S Seymour Rd.
Swartz Creek MI 48473
635.9083
4-74

If You Would Learn . . . Go Teach

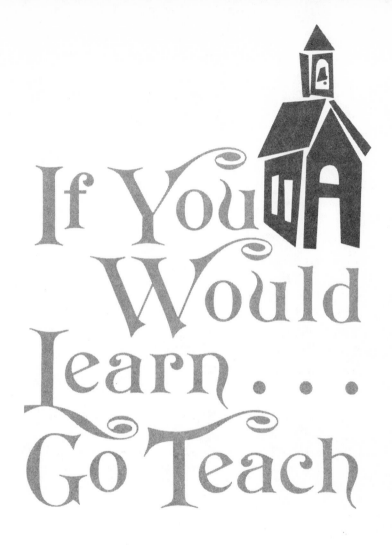

If You Would Would Learn . . . Go Teach

By Elsie Doig Townsend

COPYRIGHT © 1973
HERALD PUBLISHING HOUSE
Drawer HH
Independence, Missouri 64055

Library of Congress Catalog Card No. 73-87644
ISBN 0-8309-0105-1

Printed in the United States of America

Contents

I Choose to Teach

The truck pulled up before the small white farmhouse in Montana on a warm August morning. I was on my way across the yard, an empty milk pail swinging from each hand, coming back from the little pasture where I had been feeding the calves. The driver of the truck leaned out the window and called, "Elsie, come here, will you?"

I set down the pails and walked toward the truck.

"Good morning, Mr. Koran."

"Get in the seat here with me," he said as he swung the door open. "I want to talk to you."

I climbed up onto the high step and into the truck.

"Elsie, I never beat around the bush." He paused and looked directly into my eyes. "Why are you going away to college?"

"Because I want to be a teacher," I said. "To get a certificate I must have certain college credits."

"I am going to speak my piece. Why don't you and my son Ned get married?"

"What?"

"I mean—you like each other, don't you? All summer you've been going places together. You have grown up in the same community—known each other all your lives."

"But Mr. Koran, I—he—"

"If you'll give up this crazy notion of college I'll deed

you and Ned the Ernest Broder place that I bought last spring. It is a good ranch; it would make a good living for you."

He paused and I tried to digest what he had said.

He continued on. "I'll help you stock the little ranch, lend you machinery to run it."

"But why?"

"Because I'd like to have you for my daughter-in-law and I want Ned to settle down. He's crazy about you. Everybody knows that. If you go away he'll be wanting to leave too."

"But I have my plans all made. I have been saving money."

"You like Ned, don't you? Of course you do."

A red flush burned my face and I looked away from his probing eyes.

Defensively I mumbled, "But I want to be a teacher. I do appreciate your offer, Mr. Koran. But don't you understand?"

"Think about my offer, anyway," he said. I climbed out of the truck, and he drove away.

Two weeks later my brother took me to the train. After paying for my ticket I had very little money in my purse. My brother fished deep in his overalls pocket.

"Here," he said. "I've been saving this to give to you." He laid in my hand two twenty-dollar gold pieces.

Trying to thank him I choked up and could only give him a squeeze before I boarded the train.

For two quarters of twelve weeks each I stayed in college, doing all the housework for two families in the afternoons, evenings, and on Saturdays for income. But when the end of the second quarter came I did not have enough money to pay for my tuition for the next term. I used the little cash I had to buy a ticket to go home.

I made arrangements at the county seat to take examinations and I qualified for a teaching certificate. It was late in March, and of course there were no school openings then. So I worked on the ranch for my father.

For almost two weeks I drove eight horses on the triple gangplow. Handling four lines, raising the heavy plowshares out of the ground at the end of each furrow, and managing the horses in strung-out order soon trimmed my weight down to a neat hundred and ten pounds. The plowing done, my father set me at the harrowing. Driving six horses behind a walking harrow made me appreciate again the choice of occupation I had made—teaching. Because he was concerned about my labor, my father offered to exchange with me for a day. He was driving the wheat seeder and rode all the while.

The next day I harnessed the four horses, hooked them to the drill, lifted the hundred-pound sacks of wheat into the seeder box, and drove to the field. The horses chosen for this heavy machinery were the strongest ones on the ranch, but also the youngest. They were frisky and demanded skillful handling. It was necessary for the rows of wheat to be perfectly straight.

"Sight toward the end of the field," my father directed. "Pick out an object and aim toward it."

I tried. But the horses pranced and twisted, and I made crooked rows across the field. All morning I drove the horses on that drill. At noon I offered to trade back with my father, and returned to harrow back and forth across the plowed field until the soil was smooth.

It was June before I found a school in which there was a vacancy, a little country school west of us about fifteen miles. I was hired for the term beginning in September.

It was a typical rural school, a single-room building sitting on a lonely treeless hill not far from the community cemetery. I was eighteen years old and my oldest student was fifteen. I had twenty-five pupils in the eight grades. I stayed in a home a mile away where three of my pupils lived. The house had only one bedroom. The mother hung two big pieces of canvas between the beds. On one side was my bedroom; her husband and she and the children slept on the other side.

I walked the mile of dirt road to school, carrying a small pail of lunch and a bucket of water. It was my task to sweep the floors, carry in the coal for the little potbellied stove in the middle of the room, and carry out the ashes. On weekends I washed the blackboards and, when the mud had been heavy, scrubbed the floors.

Ignorant and untrained as I was, I made all the mistakes "in the catalog." I had the fourth-grade language class studying an old seventh-grade text for weeks before I discovered my error. But I was challenged, and I used many hours to study and learn so that I would not fail the twenty-five children.

In November I began to plan for Christmas—teaching songs of Santa Claus, rehearsing skits, plays, and recitations. In art period the older students helped the first-graders cut out Christmas trees from green construction paper and tack them on the upper frame of the blackboard. Using a stencil I had ordered from a catalog, I made the outline of Santa and his reindeer on the blackboard and filled in the picture with colored chalk. Excitement mounted each day.

Then, just a week before Christmas, a traveling preacher came to the community and began to hold a series of meetings in the dance hall near my schoolhouse. The people attended out of curiosity, a lack of entertainment, and, perhaps, religious fervor. Sunday night the hall was crowded. I was there too.

After the opening songs and prayer, the preacher read a scripture, then paused dramatically and called out, "Will all the small children come to the front of the room." Eagerly, expectantly they crowded forward, standing in rows before him.

"Now," he said, "how many of you think there's a Santa Claus?"

Without exception the children raised their hands.

"Who told you there's a Santa Claus?" he asked, thumping out each syllable.

"Mommy did," one said.

"Daddy told me."

The preacher waited until the children finished responding.

"Well, your mommy and daddy are liars. Liars, I said! There isn't any Santa Claus. And when they told you that they told you lies. Lies!" he shouted. "And you know what happens to liars? The Bible says they go to hell!"

The children began to whimper and cry. They straggled back to their parents. One little girl, weeping loudly, her fists shoved into her eyes, stood until her mother came to pick her up in her arms.

For forty minutes that preacher held us all over fire and brimstone until we could almost smell our eyebrows scorching. He was very convincing.

At school the next day, the younger children still cried and could not study. On the advice of a few families, I took down the Christmas decorations, canceled my program plans, but tried to lift the spirits of the very disillusioned little children. When school was out for the holidays, I turned the key in the lock of the schoolhouse door and hurried to my parents' home where a Christmas tree and presents warmed my frosted soul.

For two years I taught the country school, saved my money, and then went back to college. This time I was able to complete two years' work before I once again ran out of cash and had to return to schoolteaching. This time I chose western Montana where I had found a vacancy in a school located forty-five miles from town in a mountain community of ranchers.

I not only welcomed the opportunity to earn more money but also to use the knowledge I had accumulated in the college terms. I also learned to ski along the mountain sides that year, to jump the irrigation ditches on my skiis, and slide out onto the ice of the creek. With my older students I hiked the mountains on Saturdays. We explored a cave high up on the hillside, ate a meal in a sheepherder's wagon, and watched the branding. Every week I learned more than my pupils did.

The schoolhouse was a one-story white building, almost hidden in a clump of golden willows that grew along the banks of a swift mountain stream. A fence enclosed the school yard grown over with tall broom grass. The wooden teeter-totter and the tall posts of the swings poked up through the tangled summer growth. I pushed through the wooden turnstile and stepped onto the thick planks which formed a walk to the front step. The unlocked door yielded easily to a turn of the knob, and I stepped inside the room. The musty odor of closeness, of chalk dust, brought a familiar emotion—a mixture of fear, of anxiety, of excitement, of challenge. It was the first day of school.

I set my lunch pail on a shelf in the cloakroom, placed the bucket of drinking water on a bench near a white-enameled washbasin, and walked into the room. The desks had been freshly varnished, the blackboards washed clean, and the floor smelled of strong lye soap. Going to the teacher's desk, I opened drawer after drawer until I discovered a box of chalk. I began to write the program for the school day beginning at the upper left corner of the blackboard: Opening exercises 9:00-9:10; second grade reading. . . .

The children arrived in one group, all walking down the canyon road as I had come. I stood at the open door and listened to their eager chatter. As they came nearer, I categorized them according to the former teacher's class record—two second-graders, a third-grader, two fourth, two sixth, and an eighth!

In October, one of my pupils taught me much about discipline. He was a second-grader, a small wiry little fellow, but he had a vocabulary like that of a mule trainer. He could swear for minutes without repeating himself, intermingling obscenities with the cuss words.

"Jimmy," I warned again and again, "you cannot use those words here at school."

"Yes, ma'am," he would answer. "I mean, no, ma'am."

He had a fiery temper, and on the playground he flared to anger quickly when displeased. His black eyes burned as his emotions were aroused and his response to supposed insults or to defeats was a spurt of profanity and vile words.

After weeks of attempting to control this language by talking to him, I began to use threats.

"Jimmy," I warned, "the next time you use those words I am going to spank you. You understand, don't you?"

"Un-huh," he said looking up at me with those dark eyes. "I won't do it no more, honest."

Several days passed with no incident. Then, during the afternoon recess when we were out on the playground, Jimmy and a friend were on the teeter-totter. I heard one end of the wooden plank hit the ground with a sharp thud. On the other end I saw daylight between Jimmy's seat and the board. The little boy yelled out a string of swear words, his careful control giving way to fear and anger.

When his end of the teeter-totter neared the ground he slid off and ran around to the front of the schoolhouse. I started after him, but he was a quick little fellow. Out the gate he sped, fear adding strength to his legs. Across the road north and up the hill he ran with the speed of an antelope. I went after him, and behind me the other students followed. On we raced, Jimmy in the lead, I next, and the children trailing behind. We ran and ran and ran, our breath coming in gasps.

"Surely I can catch a seven-year-old," I panted to myself.

We went down that hill and around and started up a steeper one. I was puffing and wheezing. "This is absurd, absolutely unbelievable," I muttered to myself, but ran on, determined to catch the boy.

For over thirty minutes I chased that boy. All the time the other students remained strung out behind me. Finally, with a burst of speed, I grabbed the seat of his pants and hung on. He writhed and twisted, but I bent him over one knee and gave him five or six good whacks on the seat of his trousers. I was too tired to hit very hard.

"I had to do that, Jimmy," I said to him and to the children who had caught up with us.

The little boy just stood there—not even crying. Taking his hand, I started back to the schoolhouse. When we came near I said, "It's three thirty now, children. You may go home. I am going to Jimmy's home and talk with his mother."

Wearily I walked up the road—two miles and a half—to explain to the parents. Jimmy did not lose his control of his tongue again that school year—at least not where I could hear.

14

I Learn from Experience

"Miss Andes, this is Pence Powell, who owns a ranch about five miles southwest of here," my hostess explained as she introduced the tall fellow to me. He smiled and displayed white-white teeth and laughing blue eyes.

"When his divorced wife sued him for alimony, he chose to go to jail, and I took him a cake as I had promised," she added.

They laughed together.

"Did you ever pay the alimony, Pence?" she asked.

"Nope—didn't have that kind of money; just waited it out, and then I was turned loose."

"You'll stay for supper, Pence," she invited.

"You won't need to ask me twice. Bachelor cooking is terrible."

The conversation was gay, the company relaxed. After the meal we played bridge. I was partnered with Pence. With ease we lost every game, but there was no rancor. No one scolded me for my inept playing.

"I am a born loser," Pence said, "so I am used to it."

It was almost sunset the next Friday evening. I stood at the door of the schoolhouse wringing out the cloth rag with which I had been washing blackboards.

Another weekend ahead, I thought. What shall I do

besides washing my hair and doing my laundry? Wish something exciting would happen!

For six weeks I had been teaching in this little valley. Not once had I gone over ten miles from the ranch house where I boarded. It was forty-five miles to town and I had no car!

Restlessly I walked about the little schoolroom, putting out long pieces of chalk in the blackboard tray, not eager to begin the walk to the ranch house. I carried the water pail to the door and emptied it on the boardwalk, watching it run down the wooden planks and trickle into the dust where it made dark spots of instant mud.

I looked up at the mountains to the west where an early snow already covered the highest peaks, then swung my gaze to the pine-dark canyon walls on the south. A large hawk screamed across the sky and settled in the willows by the creek. Beige-colored prairie dogs scurried in and out of holes in the low dirt bank across the road.

Suddenly I heard the throb of an automobile engine. Turning toward the sound, I waited until a car appeared on the road, climbing from the valley below. It came nearer, slowed, and then stopped before the school yard.

Why, it looks like Pence Powell, I recorded mentally and walked toward the stile.

The man in the automobile reached over to turn off the motor, opened the door, and got out of the car.

"Hi, school puncher!" he said as he walked toward me. "How's it going?"

"So-so," I said without enthusiasm.

"Hey, how about going with me to Bozeman to a movie tomorrow night?"

"I—oh—uh—you surprise me by your suddenness."

"Think it over and then say yes," he said laughing.

"You have persuaded me."

"Great! I'll be over after I get the chores done tomorrow evening. Guess I better be getting home." He waved, climbed into the car seat, and drove back down the road.

In the schoolhouse, I picked up my lunch pail and went out the door. Slowly I walked up the dusty road. To town, I thought. I'm going to see electric lights, paved streets, maybe even hear a railroad train. And I quickened my steps.

Early in the morning it began to rain. The rain fell steadily all day, pounding on the trees and sending the dry aspen leaves to the ground in cascades. Gazing out through the streaming windows, I looked ruefully at the muddy road.

"Do you think Pence will come?" I asked at the supper table.

"He'll be here. He's an inveterate optimist. But those roads are bad. We've had no rain for weeks. This water mixed with dust and dry top dirt has made them what we call 'greasy.' And there'll be dangerous places in the canyon," said the ranch owner in whose home I lived.

His wife pooh-poohed the idea of real danger.

At seven o'clock the blue coupe pulled up before the yard gate. Pence scrambled out, made a run through the gate and up the walk. The rancher's wife held the door open while he stomped his feet, came through the kitchen, and strode into the dining room where we were.

"Ready to go?" he asked exuberantly as he shook the rain off his hat into the coal pail by the heating stove.

"Do you think we should?" I asked.

"Sure! Why not? Afraid of a little rain? Come on!"

Looking from the rancher to his wife and then to Pence, I hesitated a moment, then went to my bedroom to get my coat, scarf, and purse.

"I think the storm is almost over," he said. "Rain's not coming down so hard anymore."

We said good-bye and hurried out to the car. The vehicle slipped and slid as Pence turned it around in the yard and started down the dirt road. Ignoring the rain he drove, keeping the car "herded between the two fences," as he called it.

"Like to sing?" he said gaily. "How about 'My Blue Heaven'? You know that one, don't you?"

He had a light tenor, untrained but pleasing to the ear. I harmonized with him as he carried the melody.

Four or five miles below the schoolhouse he turned off onto a side road going south toward the creek.

"This way is quite a bit shorter in distance. Saves going all the way to Aberdeen Junction and then south," he explained.

Not knowing the country, I did not dissent. We went down to the little bridge across the mountain stream, rumbled across on the logs, and started up the incline on the other side. We had slowed down to cross the bridge—the individual logs were not fastened together and there was danger of one log flipping up into the air. The mud was heavy, a thick gumbo that rolled up on the wheels and collected on the underside of the fenders, impeding progress. The car wheezed to a halt.

Pence backed it down the hill, then tried going forward. The wheels spun furiously, but the car did not go ahead.

"I'll get out and give it a push. You get under the steering wheel and drive it. When I get my shoulder against the back fender I'll call out."

I slid over, put one foot on the clutch and the other on the accelerator.

"Now!" he yelled, and I roared the motor and put it into gear. Slowly we inched forward throwing great gobs of mud toward Pence! We pulled up over the rise and I stopped the car. Pence wiped his hands on an old towel above the seat and climbed in.

"How about a little stimulation?" he asked.

"From the way you're puffing, I think you have had that."

"I mean the liquid kind. Reach into the glove compartment and let's have it right now."

I reached—there I found a flat bottle which I handed to him.

"Try it," he offered. "Old Man Leasy makes the best moonshine I know of."

"I don't drink," I said primly, and pulled back into my corner of the car seat.

"Well, I do!" he said. "All the more for me."

He pulled the cork, tilted back his head, and let the liquor gurgle out of the bottle and down his throat. His Adam's apple jerked with each tremendous swallow.

"I'll save the rest for afterwhile," he said, pushing in the cork and reaching past me to deposit the bottle again in the compartment.

"Shall we try it again now? Motor's cooled down a bit."

We drove along on the level for a distance until the road again tilted sharply upward. After a few yards, the car stalled. Pence let it back down and tried again. This time we went only a few yards before it stopped, not as far up the hill as we had been before.

"The wheels are packed full of mud," he said. "I'll have to dig it out somehow."

This time, I got out of the car too, the rain matting my hair and trickling down my neck. It was dark, but Pence stumbled off into a thicket of brush and came back with two stout sticks he had cut from willow trees.

"Here," he said, giving me one. "Poke out the gumbo

from under the fenders. It's packed so full that the wheels can't turn around."

With mud sticking to our shoes until they became heavy as boots, we pushed and poked and stabbed. My stick broke in two and Pence brought another one for me.

"Now for the mud that's stuck to the tires," he directed.

The rain had soaked through my thin coat. It was a cold rain, but the exercise of scraping and poking warmed our bodies. Again and again Pence tried to drive the car up the hill. In the last attempt the car slid completely off the road and into the ditch, the motor roaring in protest. Pence turned off the switch, got out of the car, and came over to me—holding out the bottle of whiskey.

"Changed your mind? Want a little nip?"

I pushed it away. He tipped up the bottle and drank, then tossed the empty container into the ditch beside the car.

"One dead Indian joins another," he said. "Shall we start back? We have only 'shank's ponies' but they're safe and sure."

It was very dark for we no longer had the illumination of the car lights. Slipping and sliding, we followed the muddy road, feeling our way along. The continuing rain and the heavy clouds blotted out the sky and the stars. My legs ached. My shoes were very heavy. Now and then I shook my feet to throw off great chunks of mud. I was disgusted with myself—with my impulsive acceptance of Pence's offer to take me to town—with my not listening to the advice of the ranch owner.

Mile by mile we came nearer the house where I lived. As we approached the yard, the dogs came barking to meet us. I spoke to them and they quieted as soon as they recognized my voice.

At the door Pence said, "Pretty sorry affair, wasn't it?"

"It wasn't your fault. And we did not get hurt."

"I think I'll go to the bunkhouse and sleep there." He disappeared in that direction.

Carefully I pulled off my heavy, mud-caked shoes and set them inside the screened-in back porch. Walking on tiptoe I sneaked to my bedroom.

At breakfast we got it. When I walked hesitantly into the room, the ranch owner began a popular song of that era. Everyone joined him: " 'Isn't it great after being out late—walking my baby back home?' "

They stopped to shout with laughter. Pence came in and the song was repeated with gusto. It was months before I lived that down. Somehow Pence and I never had the courage to try to go to town again.

I Learn of a Small Feud

The next year I changed to a little school farther down the canyon. The valley was wider; on either side of the swift stream, the fields and pastures led up to the mountains. It was only thirty-five miles of dirt roads from town.

The schoolhouse was larger, and beside it stood a two-room teacherage where I would live. In one corner of the yard was a barn. Most of the students rode horseback to school—often one in the saddle and one behind—except in very frigid weather. I wouldn't have to carry water for drinking. Near the south fence of the school yard a gooseneck pipe rose out of the ground about two feet. A stream of cold water ran constantly from its mouth and drained away through a bed of gravel below it. The water had been piped from a nearby mountain spring.

In the front school yard was a wooden stile made of long planks which formed steps up and over the fence. Three big aspen trees—called "quakin' asp" by the natives—offered shade. There were willows out by the horse shed.

My first real domain, I thought, almost a home. Entering the teacherage, I glanced over the little low monkey stove which would do for heating and cooking, at the sink with a pail beneath, the table and two chairs, and the telephone on the wall. Moving into the room I read a placard tacked over the old-fashioned wall phone: "During severe weather, call each home after children arrive. The school district pays the phone bill."

An open doorway led to the tiny bedroom where I found a dresser, bed, and a small rocking chair—no closet, just a wire across one corner of the room. Hearing voices I hurried outside to greet the students.

Before the day was over, I discovered my problem in this school: a little social feud. The Anderson children and their friends did not associate with the Bensons and their friends. At recess I tried to organize games. No good! There was an invisible barrier between the two groups, and I was supposed to respect it. The Andersons and their coterie played in the yard that period while the Bensons drowned out gophers in the pasture across the road. Afternoon recess the groups reversed their places. I shuttled from one group to the other.

At noon I sat on the top step leading into the schoolhouse and began to unwrap a sandwich. The one group of friends sat on the east side of me, the other group on the west. No one seemed angry with any one else; the members of one group simply ignored the members of the opposite group.

I was completely baffled. It presented a challenge, but each day I became more bewildered. I tried various devices to break the feud. None worked!

"Jenny, would you and Eleanor go to the water pipe and set the bucket under the stream so it will fill?" I asked, pretending innocence of the social conflict.

"Please, Miss Andes, I'll go if Johnny can help me," Jenny said willingly.

"If Allen goes with me, I'll go," Eleanor countered smoothly.

I tried to weave new woof across the ruptured fabric of the little school community but failed with each attempt.

The children never defied me. They politely excused themselves and offered their own alternatives. I found that this was a reflection of the social lives of the families of the whole community.

After a few weeks of this, I went to town and bought a big ball of binder twine. The following Monday, at first recess, I called out, "Hey, kids, look what I have!"

"Why, that's just binder twine. What are we going to do with that here in school?" one older student said.

I went to the cloakroom and brought out a white-covered ball.

"Did any of you ever play volleyball?" I asked.

A chorus of negatives answered my question.

"Well, this is a volleyball and we are going to make our own net and play. It'll take all of us, working together, to make the net that divides the court, and we'll need every one of us to make complete teams so that we can play the game."

"Can I play too?" asked one of my first-graders.

"Yes, we'll have the net down low. Usually the game is played with nine on each side. We don't have quite that many, so we must all play. Let's go out front and I will tell you about it."

They followed me out the door and down the steps. I pointed to the aspen trees, two growing about twenty feet apart.

"How far is it from one tree to the other?"

A medley of answers came.

"I think we can tie the volleyball net to these trees *when* we get the net made. Now, we're going to tie a lot of knots—hard knots, square knots, or whatever you call them, but no granny knots. Let's see—Jennie Anderson, will you bring those big scissors from my desk drawer? Better bring two pairs! Give one pair to Howard Benson." In her eagerness to be part of the fun she ran to obey, forgetting the Benson part of the order.

"Come on, the rest of you, help me measure the length of twine we'll need for the top line of the net. It must reach from one tree to the other with a little extra to tie around the trees. Jackie Benson, take the ball and walk to the east tree; Paul Anderson, hold the end of the twine and walk to the west tree. Then each of you measure around your tree."

We began to work on the net. Sitting on the ground we measured and tied. At first the Anderson gang sat on one side, the Benson clan on the other. But the net-making involved crossing over and tying. As we worked I explained the rules of volleyball. When we wearied of rules, I told them stories. Then we played games—sitting down games which we could do with our minds as our fingers were busy with the net.

"I see something that is white with green," I said. "What is it?"

"Is it the teacherage?" someone called.

Hesitantly at first, then throwing away those foolish inhibitions they all joined in the fun. It took us several days to complete the net. Helping one little boy to shinny up a tree, we handed him one end of the long twine fastened to the top of the net. He tied it securely to the big trunk. Another tie lower down on the tree secured the bottom of the net. We repeated the process with the other end of the net.

"We're ready to play now," I said. "First we'll learn how to serve. Put the ball on your left hand and . . ." For a long time we practiced getting the ball over the net in a serve. "Now let's choose up sides. Anna, you and Joe are the tallest and the oldest. Come on and choose. Now, remember, you want the very best athletes chosen first."

These were both friends of the Bensons. Holding my breath, I waited for them to choose.

"I'll take Jennie Anderson," Anna said.

I could have shouted with joy. The first real breakthrough! Every day we played volleyball, some of the older students becoming very adept at it. Then we switched to baseball, marking out our diamond in the pasture across the road from the schoolhouse. Each day I could see some improvement in the social relationships of the feuding groups.

Somehow the children had found out the date of my birthday. I must have told them though I didn't remember it. I suppose I felt it was safe to tell them because it was not on a school day that year. During that week we had a slight earthquake which shook us enough to scare us. In Helena, the damage was quite extensive. A cowboy in the neighborhood offered to take me Saturday—the day of my birthday—to see the results of the quake. We were gone all day—one hundred and thirty miles over and back. It was dark when we stopped before my little teacherage.

"I think I see a car parked in the school yard," I said. "I'm going out there to tell those necking young people to go away."

Stumbling in the dark, I started toward the schoolhouse. Suddenly the door was flung open; light splashed out and many voices called, "Surprise! Happy birthday!"

I ran up the steps and looked into the room. It was filled with people. And there were Bensons and their friends intermingled with the Anderson family and their friends. They laughed and called to me and to each other.

Someone brought out a cake with the exact number of candles on it. Someone else lighted the candles. The children began to sing, "Happy birthday ..." and the entire crowd joined in.

"But who planned it?" I asked as we ate cake and ice cream—homemade from old wooden freezers—and drank Kool-Aid.

"We did; we all did it together," came the answer from every single one of my students, the Bensons and their friends and the Andersons and their friends.

I Learn in a Crisis

The day began with an ominous gray color. Only a faint halo of light in the east showed where the sun was hidden behind the layers of clouds. Just seven students arrived at the schoolhouse by nine o'clock, three of them accompanied by their parents.

By noon a cold northwest wind was howling down the valley, occasionally bringing stinging, icy snow with it. By two o'clock a blizzard raged outside. The sky, the mountains, trees—all were obliterated. A fine snow almost as dry as sand was driven by the raging wind.

I brought the mantle lamp from the teacherage and lighted it. We continued class recitation, but the students were restless, looking often at the windows which had begun to frost over and listening to the howling storm. At three thirty I went to the teacherage and telephoned the parents.

"I'll keep the children here at the school," I offered. "I don't think they should start home. I can't see across the school yard."

"What about food?" they asked.

"I'll manage; don't worry."

As I opened the door, the wind struck with such force that the door banged back against the wall and a gust of frigid air rushed into the room. Outside, the blinding snow, driven by the powerful wind, hid everything, even the fence around the school yard. Only the outlines of the schoolhouse were visible and it was just twenty yards from the teacherage. All faded into the oblivion of a white mist.

The students met me at the door, questioning.

"I have talked to your mothers and fathers," I said. "The storm is too severe for you to try to go home. You'll stay here tonight. Now, don't look so woebegone. I'll go put supper on to cook and then we'll have some games. Jenny, can't you read or tell a story to the younger ones?"

With difficulty I walked through the storm to the teacherage. Taking the largest pan I had, I sliced peeled potatoes into it, added water and some bits of bacon, and set it on the little monkey stove to cook. From the coal pail I filled the stove with fuel and set the dampers.

Returning to the schoolhouse, I went to the basement and began to stoke the furnace. With long poker and shovel I took out red-hot clinkers which I dropped into an empty coal pail. I shook down the ashes, carried several great lumps of coal from the bin, and piled them in the fire in the furnace.

Up in the schoolroom again I found strangely quiet children.

"How about a game of 'I Spy'? I'll be It first. I'll use this big red eraser. Now everybody go into the library room. Count to twenty and then come back."

In a few minutes they were excitedly trying to find the hidden object. When that game was worn a bit thin, I began another. We ciphered on the blackboard, the older students helping me judge, check results, and encourage the younger pupils. The roar of the wind was forgotten. We laughed and shouted and contested.

"I must go to the teacherage to finish supper," I said. "You older pupils, find a story in a book for me to read to all of you when I return, will you?"

As I stepped out the door, a gust of wind almost tipped me over. Bending forward against the strength of the storm, I ran to the shelter of the teacherage. I stirred the cooked potatoes—added butter, salt, and canned milk—tasted, and added again.

Lighting a coal oil lantern, I set it on the table by the window. In my coat pocket I stuffed spoons and forks. I buttered slices of bread, slapped them together, and slid them into a brown paper sack. In another sack I put three large cans of peaches and a can opener. It was awkward carrying all these things and the pan of potato soup, but I managed to get the door open and shut after me. Once more I fought through the wind and snow to the schoolhouse. My pounding on the door brought the older students to open it.

"Each one get his tin cup from the nails in the entry," I called out gaily. "We are going to eat supper."

Setting the pan of soup on the big hot furnace register in the middle of the room, I dipped and poured the soup into their cups. I handed out spoons and forks.

"Girls, here are bread and butter sandwiches for each one," I said pointing to the sack.

Hungrily we ate, sitting at our desks, laughing. The strange experience became intriguing rather than frightening. Opening the tin cans, I set them on the teacher's desk, and each pupil helped himself to the golden fruit, spooning it into his tin cup.

"You can have a drink of water as soon as we wash our cups. I'll have to bring over a pan of water that is heating on the teacherage stove. Now, if you want to go to the john, take turns using the girls'—it's the nearest. None of you younger students are to go out alone. Jean, you stand by the back door and guard its opening and closing, will you? Don't let it flip back nor be open too long. I'll be back in a jiffy."

This time I carried the lantern with me when I returned, bringing a bucket of hot water and towels. Pulling the desks around in a circle, we sat near the lamp. From a book written by Schultz—one of their favorite writers—the students had chosen a story for me to read to them. One of the eighth-graders took turns with me as we read on and on. For an hour or more there was very little sound except the howling wind outside and the reading inside. One of the youngest children laid his head on his desk.

"It's time to figure out a way to sleep. I think I know what we can do," I suggested. "I have a tarpaulin and an old blanket that we'll spread on the floor. There's a clean dry mop hanging on the wall halfway down the stairs to the basement. Bill, you rub the dust off the floor all around the register."

When I returned from the teacherage, we laid the tarp on one side of the register, the blanket on the other.

"Now bring all your coats and wraps. Put on your snow pants. We'll spread our coats over us to keep us warm. You three boys lie on the north side. Jennie, you and the two littlest girls can sleep in my bed in the teacherage. I'll sleep here with Eleanor on the south side of the register."

The strangeness of the experience was exciting. We scurried about getting ready for the night. I went with the girls to the teacherage, helped them get settled, and filled the stove. In the large pan I poured out a sack of dry beans and filled the pan with water.

I went to the schoolhouse basement again to refill the furnace. By the time everyone was bedded down, it was getting late. The boys talked awhile, then lay listening to the storm until they dropped off to sleep.

I had left a kerosene lamp burning low in the teacherage. Now I blew out the mantle lamp and turned down the wick of the lantern. Every two hours or so during the night I tended the furnace—refueling it, shaking it, and keeping the fire burning high. Twice, I plodded through the storm to the teacherage and poured coal in the stove there.

Toward morning the roar of the wind began to abate somewhat, but the snow still whirled, blotting out everything but the teacherage. It was bitter cold.

I cooked a big pan of cereal—oatmeal—and we ate cups of it with condensed milk serving as cream. At nine o'clock we began our classes. For recess we put on coats and went to the basement where we played lively games of tag and Blindman's Buff.

At noon we ate bean soup, crackers, and fruit. By afternoon the storm had lulled. I called the parents at three o'clock. They started out to meet their children.

The younger students I helped bundle up into their snow pants, overshoes, heavy coats, and caps. I tied the long scarves around their necks, pulled one layer of the woolen cloth over their faces up to their eyes, and checked to see that mittens were on.

Standing at the window, I watched them begin the walk along the drifts of snow. In places the hard-crusted drifts hid the fences completely. I did not relax until each parent had called to say that his child was safely home.

I Learn of Life and Death

Each spring, at the end of the school term, I packed my belongings and headed for college. During the summer I earned credits toward a degree in education. In the fall I returned to teaching to pay for college expenses and to try to save a little for the next year.

The fellow to whom I had become engaged was attending an art school in Saint Paul. We planned to get married in a year or two, but we had agreed that we must have some social life where we lived.

During the third year of my teaching in the valley, I took correspondence courses from the university. I had counted credits very carefully with the registrar and I figured I could graduate the following summer. My evenings were filled with studying and writing out my lessons.

One Saturday morning as I carried the dishwater out of the teacherage and threw it into the ditch at the side of the road, I stood looking up at the mountain nearest the school yard. The sun peeked around the side of its gigantic rocky crest, lighting up its dark forests, the sheer rocky precipices of its front side, and the sloping foothills below. Bright splashes of golden aspen trees contrasted with the green of the firs and pines. I began to quote, "I will lift up mine eyes unto the hills, from whence cometh . . ."

I was distracted by the rumble and roar of a car. At the

head of a great puff of dust it approached the school yard and stopped with a jerk, the cloud of dust catching up with it and settling over the strange-looking, topless vehicle.

I stood gazing at the car—a queer put-together thing—the seat just a plank over the gas tank, no windshield, a sort of half-truck back. The engine hood was wired on; there were no fenders over the rear wheels, no running board. A laugh gurgled up inside me. I choked it quickly when I saw the driver scramble out of this makeshift conveyance and walk toward the school fence where I remained staring in wonder and amazement.

"Miss Andes, the teacher, aren't you?" he questioned and tipped his head.

"Yes," I answered and waited.

"I'm Jim Doig. Just moved into the Poison Hollow Ranch this fall—you know, the place up near the top of Horseshoe Hills." He motioned to the west with his head.

"Oh, yes," I said.

"Uh—er—can I take you to the Pinetree School Dance Friday night?"

For a second I was speechless. The audacity! I thought. Who does he think he is? Why, I've never even met him before.

"I don't think I want to go," I said baldly. "Besides I am busy with some college courses that I study at night."

"You don't think you might change your mind?"

"Not likely!"

"Well, I'll see you again."

He seemed not at all abashed, but walked quickly toward his car. He moved purposefully—as if he had things to do. I stood watching him. He was tall, broad-shouldered, narrow-hipped, and walked with the typical gait of a cowboy in high-heeled boots. He turned and waved as he drove away. I had a glimpse of his rugged features, his smile a flash of white teeth.

"Humph!" I said aloud. "The nerve of him! Well, that's one homely cowboy I'll not go anywhere with. He'll not bother me again."

And I turned to go to the teacherage. But the next Saturday he stopped again.

"Would you go with me to the farewell party the community is having for the Jones family?" he asked, as lightheartedly as if I had not turned him down before.

"No, thank you," I said primly, not even giving an excuse.

He stood a few moments, talking of the weather, of the cattle on the upper pastures. Then he tipped his hat and went back to his patched-up vehicle.

That evening, when I walked to the Morgan ranch a quarter of a mile away to get some milk, I decided to ask about this persistent fellow.

"Yeah, Jim Doig," Hank Gordon said. "I know him. Young bachelor that brought his cattle down Haw Gulch from the country north of Sixteen Mile Canyon to the Horseshoe Hills. He rents Poison Hollow Ranch. Those people that own it have retired and live in Arizona. The house and barns and corrals are about four miles away at the base of a narrow canyon leading toward the top of the mountain. Lots of pasture and some hay land."

"This fellow lives all alone?"

"Yep! He's a-batchin' it. Say, school puncher, he'd make a purty good catch for some single teacher I know." And he laughed and slapped his leg.

The next week Jim Doig stopped again at the teacherage. Once more I refused his offer. I had resolved not to accept. But we stood by the fence and talked for quite a while.

Robert Burns had words for it: "The best laid schemes of mice and men gang aft agley." The fourth invitation I accepted. I found his Scottish humor refreshing, his brogue intriguing, and his car very hard to ride in.

"*Sklester,* you said. What's that mean?" I asked.

He laughed easily. "Oh, that's Scottish for 'a mess, a general confusion.' "

"Your parents were from Scotland?"

"Both of them, but Father's dead. Does my speech sound odd to you? We have always lived in the Wall Mountain community. All of the people there are from Scotland. They homesteaded that area at the turn of the century. I was born and grew up there."

"You used the expression 'steppin harness.' Is that Scottish?"

"Oh, no! that's a cowboy's way of saying getting dressed up in his best clothes."

"And what are cackleberries?" I asked.

"Eggs! You can figure out how that word came about, can't you?" And he laughed.

He was easy to be with. I continued to go with Jim to the community social affairs. I wrote my fiancé about him.

One Saturday we packed our lunch, stowed it in a pack to carry over our shoulders, and drove to the base of the nearest mountain, the one that shadowed my school yard. Leaving the car at the end of the road, we started to climb to the top of the mountain. Toughie, Jim's favorite cow dog went with us. For hours we toiled up the steep incline, in one place going a long way around a perpendicular rocky cliff that was impossible for us to climb. At times we were in such a dense growth of trees that we could see nothing but our immediate vicinity.

"I've heard the statement 'can't see the forest for the

trees,' but I never quite understood the complete meaning before," I said as we sat on rocks and breathed deeply.

When we reached the top, we stood gazing in every direction.

"Look! There are the mountains of the continental divide just beyond Helena," I said pointing to the northwest.

Jim gestured to the west. "If you look carefully you can see the ribbon of the Missouri River coming out of the gorge near Cardston, many miles away."

To the south I recognized the Spanish Peaks, then the mountains of Yellowstone Park about a hundred and fifty miles away. I turned another ninety degrees. Again I pointed.

"Is that the valley down below Fairy Lake, behind Sacajawea Mountain?"

Jim's eyes followed my pointing finger.

"Yes," he said, "and northeast, the mountains beyond White Sulphur Springs."

We drank in the majesty and wonder of the scene while we ate our lunch. Then we began our descent. The shale rock tore the leather hide of my shoes as we slid and walked down the great slides.

In the spring I took off my engagement ring and sent it to the fellow I had promised to marry. When I finished that summer term at college I was graduated. Ten days later Jim and I were married. For six years we lived in the ranch near the top of the Horseshoe Hills, where I had first a daughter, then a set of twins, then another set of twins. Three months after the last twins were born, Jim was thrown from a horse and severely injured. He died five days later.

Neighbors helped round up the cattle and sell them. I sold the saddle horses, the saddles, and the work horses to pay all the debts. Taking my five babies, I moved to a little mountain town about ninety miles away and began to teach.

That Math Teacher

I had noticed her the first day I entered the school in September. She walked quickly past my door—not hurriedly, just determinedly—as if she anticipated her day and enjoyed the anticipation. This brief glimpse of her revealed an old dark-blue dress that hung unevenly on a dumpy figure, gray hair in a short, mannish cut, and steel-rimmed glasses which reflected the light coming from my classroom windows as she passed my open door. Cleaning woman, I thought, as I looked down at my stylish brown dress and matching shoes.

But I was wrong. When we filed into the home economics room for the teachers' meeting, there she was. I sat looking at her until the principal began to speak.

"If each of you will stand and tell his or her name and department, we'll be getting acquainted. Miss Werner, you've been here the longest. You start it."

She stood quickly with that all-in-one movement, smiled, and spoke distinctly, "Ruth Werner, math." Her head bobbed so that the light played on her glasses as she sat down.

My surprise must have been written on my face, for the teacher beside me nudged my ribs gently and whispered, "A queer one, but you'll like her." The teacher speaking stroked her fashionable red suit. "She's an institution in this school. Been here for years and years. She wears well."

For weeks after that I was busy finding my way around

the school building, learning to know my students, my classes, and the other teachers. I was afraid of making mistakes because this was my first year of teaching in high school. I wanted to learn, wanted to fit into this school. I had to make good. My future—my children's future—depended on it.

The surrounding country was beautiful, with towering mountains already snowcapped, cold swift streams, and lakes of crystal clear water. The little town was isolated from the valley except for the one highway that twisted like a ribbon up the tortuous turns of the mountain pass south of us, over, and down the other side. There was not even a railroad into the town. It was a trading place for the ranchers who lived round about.

The days went by easily, linked to each other in a chain of learning. I had much knowledge to accumulate, more than my students. For long hours every night after my own children were asleep I studied texts. During the days I studied the ways of high school students, the customs and procedures of the school. I tried to learn about the teachers and to learn from them also. It was October before I found out much about Miss Werner.

Indian summer had come with its golden days. No one accustomed to fall in high altitude was deceived by the warmth and the sunshine which gave no hint of the not-too-distant approach of early winter. Snow might fall any night, loading the branches with its weight, hiding the bright color of the aspen trees. But each day was savored and enjoyed completely. The sky was blue-blue, with patches of thin clouds showing through like lacy petticoats. Such days would tempt any red-blooded boy of the community to go hunting.

The first day of grouse season came. Two boys were

absent from my first-hour English class. Three more were out of my third-hour class. One boy in particular could not afford to play hookey if he expected to get a passing grade. In reporting these absences to Mr. Smith, the guidance director, I said, "These boys should be warned. Their grades can't stand much of this truancy."

"First day of grouse season," he mumbled as he wrote the names on his scratch pad. "Yours isn't the only class they have skipped. Think I'll talk to Miss Werner. She'll know how to cope with them."

The following morning Mr. Smith stopped by my door long enough to call in, "Don't lower those boys' grades for yesterday's truancy. We have a better plan," and then his long legs took him rapidly on down the hall to his office.

Curious about this, I waylaid Miss Werner in the hall at noon. As she spoke to me her smile lighted up her blue eyes behind the steel-rimmed spectacles. I put my hand out to stop her when she started to hurry on after a quick greeting.

"Oh, Miss Werner, did you talk to those boys?"

"Who? Oh, yes." She spoke quickly, almost sharply. "They'll not do it again." Her smile took away any sting of rebuff. Without any more explanation she moved rapidly on to her room.

Watching her, I wondered what influence that small, unimpressive-looking teacher could have on those boys. Inwardly I criticized her rusty-black suit which sagged on both sides and the worn collar of the white blouse that drooped from lack of starch. How could that little old maid know about boys? What kind of teacher could she be? What did it take to make a good teacher?

But the boys did not skip school again in spite of the weather-perfect mornings of the wild duck season which followed soon after grouse hunting.

One afternoon the "honk-honk" of wild geese drew our eyes to the classroom window. I stopped in mid-sentence as we watched with fascination the large triangle of dark bodies flying toward the mountain lake about two miles away. The schoolhouse stood on a hill near the edge of town. From the windows we caught a flash of sunlight on the water of the lake. The echelon of geese banked, turned, and were soon lost to our view in the brush near the lakeshore.

"Will they stay there all night?" I caught myself breaking into the thoughts of the class.

"Yup," a tall senior answered instantly, "and they're big 'uns, too. Canadian geese. Up at daybreak with a good shotgun a fellow could soon git his limit."

"How many are allowed?" I knew I should get back to English, but it was near the end of the last period.

"Two," several voices said at once.

"Can you start shooting at any time?"

The bell rang to end the discussion, but one boy waited a moment to answer my question. Scraps of conversation drifted back to me as the class pushed its way down the hall.

"You going, Tom?"

"Course, but we gotta make it back 'fore nine in the morning. I promised Miss Werner. Trig's not easy for me, and I need it if I'm gonna take engineering in college."

"Let's go talk to her."

"I'm goin' anyway, no matter what she says," one voice said belligerently.

The idea of that midget teacher influencing these big six-footers seemed ridiculous. Many of them were rough-looking fellows who lived on the ranches in the vicinity. How could a teacher's control continue beyond the school hours? What did it take?

As the boys straggled into my first-hour class the next

day, wild geese were the principal topic before the bell rang.

"Git one, Bill?"

"Naw, guess the sun was right in my eyes. How 'bout you?"

"Yeah, first shot. And is he a beauty! Mom's gonna dress him and put him in the freezer. Taste good for Christmas. Hey, Red, any luck?"

"Got two, but, boy, did I get wet! Stepped in a hole and went in over my boots." He slapped his damp levi's. "Mom said to change clothes, but I told her I'd promised Miss Werner I'd make it here by nine. 'Bout dried out now."

If I could only get that kind of interest in English from them! Searching frantically through the literature book, I looked for a story or poem on hunting or on wildlife. My attention was drawn to "To a Waterfowl," and with a little introduction about the wild duck flying against the setting sun, I began to read:

> Whither midst falling dew
> While glow the heavens with the last steps of day,
> Far through their rosy depths
> Dost thou pursue thy solitary way?

I explained the unfamiliar expressions. "Durned old poetry" as the boys called it was not so hard for them if I made it come alive in a real-life situation. By the time I had reached the last stanza the students were in a somewhat pensive mood and did not even feel affronted by the "teachy-preachy" ending:

> He who from zone to zone
> Guides through the boundless sky thy certain flight
> In the long way that I must tread alone
> Will lead my steps aright.

The morning after the first snow fell I met Miss Werner in the hall.

"Beautiful snow!" she said in way of greeting. Her smile was infectious. "Marvelous deer hunting weather. Good tracking! Watch those boys. I'll try to get around to seeing all of them sometime today. If Bill Goodin doesn't show up, let me know." And she was on her way toward her room at the end of the hall.

Thank goodness it was Friday!

Saturday afternoon the children and I walked down to the ranger station office near the bridge over the river which bordered the east side of town to watch the cars as they stopped at the station to be checked. Slung across the radiator hood of a car would be a perfect two-year-old buck, or tied to the bumpers might be a five-point deer. Often there were two—one tied over the top of the car. Sometimes I recognized high school boys who poked their heads out the car windows and called out about their luck. I moved closer to the station to see the person to whom they were speaking. Miss Werner—I might have known!

Monday morning I saw a group of fellows down at the end of the hall, all talking at once, clustered around the little math teacher. As I stood watching, I tried to understand her power over these boys, the rapport they shared. Her face was transfigured with her joy and interest. To each boy she seemed to ask the right question. She spoke their language. Each fellow vied with the others to tell of his experiences. Perhaps this was the reason for her success.

In the weeks that followed, the snow became deeper and deeper. It became increasingly difficult to teach the last period of the school day. Each day fifty or more students packed the large classroom across the hall and spilled over into the corridor. My class drooled enviously as they watched skis being rubbed with wax and boots pulled on. I found out that anyone with study hall that period could sign up for this ski class. Our science teacher had been a national junior ski champion. Teaching this class was real joy for him.

Not until the students, skis over their shoulders, had clomped noisily down the hall, climbed into the station wagons, and taken off for the hills could I draw the attention of my class to the prosaic subject of English.

On Saturdays everyone who could be free drove to the ski-jump hill. Children skied on the gentle slopes. The adults came expertly down the steep hills, following the flags of the slalom, or swiftly along the track to the jump, soaring into the air, and dexterously landing hundreds of feet away. Those of us who could not ski well watched and enjoyed the sport vicariously. The whole community turned out.

Two weeks before Christmas holidays were to begin, a local ski meet was held. Businessmen of the town offered prizes. No one missed this event. Even teachers who did not attend any other local gatherings turned up that morning, dressed in their heaviest jackets and snow pants, armed with warm blankets and thermos bottles of hot coffee. My children and I rode with a neighbor. The ten miles up the canyon road had been cleared by the big rotary plow which chewed up the drifts of deep snow and piled them high along the roadside. The bright sun dazzled my vision but gave no warmth as its rays reflected from the white earth covering. People hurried out of their cars and crowded as near the ski lift as possible, their breath making little cloudlike puffs as they called greetings to each other. Some of the men tended an open fire piled with huge logs. The pungent aroma of burning fir branches filled the air. Youngsters crowded around, holding mittened hands toward the flames.

Shouts of laughter heralded an ignominious flop of a skier into the snow. A sudden hush meant that a skier was in the air off the big jump, then shouts and exclamations as he landed upright on his skis and braked to a stop. It was during one of my frequent trips to the fire to warm my fingers and check up on my children that I heard a groan from the group of watchers. Turning I looked toward the ski jump. At its base a crumpled figure made a dark blotch on the white snow of the mountainside. Several skiers moved quickly toward the figure. There was a babel of voices, some hushed, some imperatively loud with commands.

"Bring the stretcher!"

"Who is it?"

"What happened?"

"Bring the toboggan. On the double!"

Carefully the injured skier was brought down the hill, but as he was lifted onto the stretcher I saw that one leg dangled crazily. It was only a matter of minutes before he was eased into the back of a station wagon. The driver was in the seat, the motor running, and yet the car waited. Someone was calling toward the crowd, "Miss Werner, oh, Miss Werner!"

The shabby little teacher separated herself from the crowd and moved quickly across the snow to the car. In a moment she was inside and the station wagon went slowly down the narrow canyon road.

"Why did she go with them?" I inquired of a fellow standing by.

"Bill asked for her," he explained curtly as if any other answer was unnecessary.

All the way back to town I thought of the incident and what it would mean to be chosen as Miss Werner had been. In his agony of pain and anxiety, Bill turned to her. Why? That evening I went to get my mail. The post office room was filled with people, pushing and jostling each other to get to their boxes. There was much talking about the day's activities. I listened. Bill had been taken to the hospital in the valley below. His leg was broken—a spiral fracture which left the bone shattered. It had required a lengthy operation. Miss Werner and the boy's father were still with Bill.

"What about his mother?" I asked someone standing near.

"She's been dead since Bill was a small boy. Didn't you know? Bill's father has taken care of the boy alone."

At school on Monday morning I stood in the hall watching the students come and go. I heard the usual buzz of excited voices and scraps of conversation about the ski meet and Bill. Miss Werner's faded coat appeared around the corner at the regular time. Briskly she walked down the hall, her head bobbing now and then as she greeted students. No change in her attitude. She fumbled for keys in her old leather purse, unlocked her door, and went into her room. Determined to know more about this woman, I went down the hall, weaving my way in and out of the groups of students. I tapped on her door. With her call of "Come" I entered. She continued to sort some papers on her desk as she looked inquiringly at me.

"Miss Werner," I said with no preface, "please tell me how to do it."

"Do what?" she said simply. Her friendly smile encouraged me to go on.

"Tell me the secret of your success with the students. Why do they obey you? What control have you over these students, especially the boys?"

"Oh, it's easy, really. I just love them—all of them, from the biggest, roughest cowboy to the littlest, most unkempt urchin—and I let them feel it."

"But how, why?"

"Please sit down, Mrs. D., and I'll try to explain as well as I can. I've always loved children, particularly boys. When I was a girl, I planned to have a family of boys of my own after I had married. But I never married, you know. I was engaged to a young fellow when I was a senior in teachers college. We kept putting off the date for our marriage. First my mother died after a long, very expensive illness. I taught school to pay the hospital and doctor bills. Then my father's stroke left him partially helpless, and he lived with me for twenty years before he died. Of course I could not marry and leave him. But I found that I did not need to be married to have a family of boys. I have had hundreds of them in my classrooms—every school day I have them. I was not long in discovering that high school students need loving. I am partial to boys who have had broken homes and those who have been neglected. In many ways I could make up for some of the lack of love, even lack of discipline. Oh, it's not been difficult. I've enjoyed my big family of boys. What a beautiful, full life I have had!"

She stopped and smiled ruefully. "There's not much of a secret, I'm afraid. If I have had any success it has been due to my interest in these students—real interest, not just a superficial one. I care what they do and what happens to them. I really do love them."

She picked up a book from her desk and began to leaf through it.

"Thank you, Miss Werner," I said. Humbled I went back to my work of teaching, a work glorified now by a little math teacher.

Bobby

His bright red curly hair attracted my attention the first day of band practice. Brown freckles splattered over a lightly tanned face that crinkled into a broad smile when anyone spoke to this boy with a shiny French horn. I called the roll and he answered to the name of Bobby Turner. Soon I was aware of the skill with which he played his instrument.

"You like to play your horn, don't you?" I asked him when we had a break in the practice hour.

He grinned and ducked his head.

Thirteen-fourteen years old, I judged mentally. Pretty good for his age.

Every Monday, Wednesday, and Friday I noticed the boy bending over his French horn before the practice began, often lipping the notes without the use of the stops. Sometime before snow came, Bobby's mother, Polly, invited me and my children to come to dinner one Saturday. She had discovered that she was related to their father.

While we visited, Bobby took my brood out into the yard and played Hide and Seek with them. Their laughter floated in through the open windows. The big cow dog barked and ran with them.

Bobby came running into the house. "Mom, can I take colored movies of them?"

He took the camera and went out again. When his mother called dinner, the children ran to me.

"He's fun, Mama! He makes us laugh. He put on a big bear's hide and pretended he was a bear."

In February, at a PTA meeting, Polly came across the room to talk to me.

"Is Bobby having trouble playing his horn?" she asked.

"Not that I have noticed."

"He's having difficulty zipping his jacket and his over-shoes," she explained. "The ends of his fingers are not sensitive."

By March he was dragging his feet when he walked. His parents took him to the local doctor, then to a specialist in another state.

"A distrophy of the nerves, was the doctor's diagnosis," they told me.

"What can be done?" I asked.

"Nothing!" his mother said.

I looked at her quickly. The hopelessness was in her face as well as her voice. Bobby dropped out of band but finished the school year.

In May his parents moved from the community and settled in the large town in the valley where there was access to the best doctors. It was four years before I saw Bobby again when I began to teach in the high school in that town, but I had heard now and then of his gradual decline.

Soon after I began the school year, his mother called.

"Elsie," she said, "would you have time to help Bobby with his lessons? He's taking correspondence courses, trying to obtain his high school diploma."

"Of course!" I said quickly. "What evening shall I come?"

"How about Monday?"

I was not prepared for what I saw when I entered their house that night. In the middle of the living room was a hospital bed. Stretched out on it was a long figure. I could tell it was Bobby by the red hair, although it was no longer bright and curly, but dull and limp. Orange freckles made splotches of color on the chalky-white face. His feet reached the extreme end of the long bed, but with the toes drawn under they looked like clenched fists.

"Hel-lo," he said in two, slow syllables. "Sor-ry to both-er you, but I don't under-stand these dir-ections."

He reached bony, crooked fingers to a book beside him.

"What page?" I said, trying to make my voice natural.

His mother brought a packet of long, typed pages.

"These are the lessons," she said, "but I only finished eighth grade and I'm confused by these instructions."

For two hours Bobby and I studied. His eyes were bright and eager. He could lift his head a little and turn it to the right or left.

"I can write it later," he said slowly. "I'll remember all of it. I'm sure I understand what I am to do and how to do it. Thanks a lot!"

"Call me any time you get stuck," I said when I told him good-night.

Several times during the school year I went to see Bobby. Always he had questions saved up to ask. But each visit saddened me. He was weaker, too tired to use his hands much.

One Saturday that summer Polly came to our house alone. As soon as she was inside the living room, she sank into a chair and let her head rest on her hands. Alarmed I walked quickly to her.

"What is it, Polly?" I said. "Is Bobby . . .?"

For a few moments she did not speak. She did not cry—just sat with her hands over her face. Then slowly she began to talk.

"Yes, it's Bobby. The doctor was at the house just now. 'Not much longer,' he said. Bobby's failing fast."

She sat quietly for a few moments.

"And I'm so tired. I have lost all hope."

I put my hand on her shoulder and waited.

"I didn't want him to see me like this," she said.

"Is he alone?"

"No. A group of young people from the church near us were with him. They come often—to talk to him—to pray for him. They're from that queer church, but they are so kind to him. They love him."

"I'm glad."

Slowly she rose to her feet and began to button her coat.

"I must go now. He's so completely helpless."

Inanely I tried to mumble comforting syllables as I followed her out the door and to her car.

Bobby did not call me to help him with his studies again. He was too weak to hold a book; even talking over the telephone tired him.

Sometime during the late summer something began to happen—a miracle, the doctor called it—an answer to prayers the young church friends said. Slowly, almost imperceptibly—and yet definitely—Bobby began to recover. His heartbeat became strong and the rate normal. His appetite increased daily. His arms and hands regained strength.

In answer to his mother's call one day, I went to see his improvement. He was sitting in bed, propped up with pillows. His skin had a healthy glow. He moved his long legs back and forth.

"How do I look now, Elsie?" he said. "Are you surprised?"

"You look great to me," I repeated again and again.

"Dad and Mom are taking me to the hospital next week. The doctor is going to do some surgery on my feet. I think I can begin to walk again as soon as he gets my toes and ankles straightened out."

His mother hovered over him, her eyes filled with a warm glow of happiness.

Months later I saw him again—this time in a wheelchair, proudly rolling it across the floor.

"Next it's crutches," he called to me gaily. "Another trip to the hospital should do it."

Later that year, his father brought Bobby to visit us. Slowly the young fellow maneuvered himself from the seat of the car into the wheelchair his father had brought from the trunk and unfolded on the walk beside the car. Proudly Bobby manipulated the chair up the walk and onto the yard to some lawn furniture.

"I'm almost ready to get my high school diploma," he announced.

Eagerly he talked of his future—of college classes in the fall.

The next time I saw him he was walking with two canes, awkwardly, jerkily, but with determination.

I saw him once again. I had gone to his home to pick up "windfall" apples that Polly could not use. I heard a car drive up beside the yard.

"Hi!" the driver called.

Setting down my pail of apples, I went to the driveway. It was Bobby.

"Surprised? Dad got me this little car a couple of months ago. It handles so easily. I'm on wheels now!"

He opened the car door and stood on the sidewalk, not even a cane to support him.

"You'd never guess what I am doing!"

His mother had called to give me the news, but I wanted him to tell me himself.

"What?"

"I have a job. I'm the new mail carrier on a rural route that goes out into the country—north—about twenty miles around the route. Dad went with me the first few weeks. Now I can do it alone. It feels great to be on my own."

He climbed back into the car.

"Must get down to the post office and turn in these mailbags."

I stood a moment watching him drive away, then turned back to my apple picking, thrilled to have been an observer of such drama.

Learning Real Values

Doris turned the streamer of purple crepe paper over and over again, her eyes on the rows of other streamers hanging from the ceiling of the school gym.

"Twisted enough, Ben?" she called to a boy on a tall stepladder, waiting with hammer and tacks to fasten the streamers to a board let down from the high beams.

"Yeah—no, give her another turn or two. That's okay. Pass it up." And he leaned over to retrieve the long strip of paper Doris held up to him.

I saw their hands touch and his hand quickly withdrawn.

"Hey, Doris, you coming to the prom?" a voice called from the other end of the gymnasium.

"Guess not! You know how it is."

"Aw, Randy wouldn't care if you went to the prom."

"But it wouldn't be fair. Randy's in the service and . . ." She glanced at the ring on her third finger. The light flashed from the stone as she twisted another streamer. I watched her and tried to imagine her thinking.

The sound of voices surged around her, but her thoughts seemed to torment her. Why shouldn't I go? It's my junior year, and I've worked so many hours on this prom. But no one will ask me, not when I'm wearing Randy's ring.

Her thoughts brought a mental picture of Randy—his hair in a short crew cut, his crooked, irresistible smile, his teasing eyes, his devil-may-care attitude, his opposition to all rules and discipline. He was so different—so exciting to be out with. Yet sometimes he had embarrassed her by his rough remarks and by his drinking.

The teachers had been glad to see him enlist she was sure. Her parents had been, too, though they had never expressed it aloud.

"Hey, Doris, what are you dreaming about? We're going to call it quits. It is ten o'clock."

"Let's sweep up this paper. The janitors will be wrathy if they find the gym cluttered like this," I warned.

"Who knows how to turn out the lights?"

"I do," shouted Ben as he dragged the heavy ladder across the floor.

"Hey, wait a minute till I get these brooms put away."

I stood at the door waiting until everyone had left and started down the street. They straggled along in groups, all but Ben and Doris who were alone just ahead of me.

"Walking home alone?" he asked as he moved toward her.

"I live so close, Ben," she said.

"Care if I come along? It's on my way."

She turned to wait until his long strides brought him even with her.

Ben was so quiet always—bashful, you might call him. He never dated and seemed too shy to talk to the girls alone. Tonight as I walked behind him and Doris I could hear him discussing that "heck of a" test in geometry tomorrow.

Doris' hand touched her gate.

" 'Night Ben. Be seeing you."

" 'Night, Doris," he said, but he stood by her gate until she opened her door. She turned, saw him there, and waved her hand. He nodded his head and went on.

In English class next day I saw their glances lock several times. A dark red color stained Ben's face the last time, and he looked down at his book.

After school Doris followed the class as they streamed into the gym to put on the finishing touches. The girls fastened the paper flowers onto the wishing well and twined the green paper around the posts. The boys finished the structure of the queen's throne and called for help with the crepe paper that was to drape it. Doris looked at the throne and paused in her work.

"Betty will look beautiful sitting there tonight," she said, more to herself than to me. I sensed Doris' preoccupation.

"We bought our formals together in Butte during the Christmas vacation," she went on. "That was before I knew Randy would decide to enlist. If he hadn't been mixed up in the gang that broke into the pool hall that night and made away with those cases of beer, he might still be here."

"I know," I offered.

Doris' face burned. She recalled his stubborn refusal to admit he was sorry. Signing up for enlistment was the easy way out.

"The boys did a good job on the wicket fence in front of the orchestra stand, didn't they?" I commented.

She nodded and smiled.

"And the music is going to be the best!"

"Don't tempt me," she said, "or should I say 'torture'?" Have you seen the programs?"

"Have I? Ben and I worked for hours designing them in the library last week."

"Even if Randy were here, I wouldn't have much use for the program because he won't let me dance with any one else. I'd miss most of the dances entirely because he would insist on sitting out in the car and . . ."

She was so busy with her thoughts that she was unaware of the students leaving until the room was almost quiet. She looked up and saw Ben standing near, fiddling with a pair of pliers.

"Doris!" His voice sounded queer in the echoing gymnasium. He began again. "Doris, I know I'm not much of a dancer, but I can try. I don't think Randy would care if you were to come to the prom with me. I'm sure he wouldn't consider me any competition. Besides, we've known each other all our lives."

"Why, Ben, are you inviting me to the prom?"

"Yes, I can't think of your missing it. You've always loved dancing so much. If you could—" His voice trailed off. He looked at her.

"Thanks, Ben. I—I will—yes, I will." Her voice was stronger with each assertion.

"No kidding?"

Even from my waiting place over by the door I could hear the lilt in his voice.

"What color is your—er—I mean what color corsage should I get?"

"Almost any color; my dress is pale blue." She smiled up at him. She hadn't noticed he had grown so tall. They had been the same height in eighth grade.

"Shall I pick up the program and exchange the dances or will you?" There was hesitancy in his voice now.

Doris understood. The boys would ridicule him. Ben, the fellow who would never look at a girl, asking another fellow's girl! Wouldn't they rib him!

"It might be better for me to do it, Ben. I know all the couples so well," she offered.

"Okay. I'll hurry downtown to see about that corsage. Eight o'clock be all right?"

"Fine. See you," and her brown eyes danced as she ran past me at the door.

I watched for them to enter the gym that night at the prom. She held her chin high, expecting the teasing of her classmates. He walked beside her, his bent elbow close to his side, her hand slipped through the crook of his arm. His expression was passive until he glanced at her upturned face; then his features glowed with happiness.

The fluffy skirts of blue tulle swished around her ankles. How much fun she was having wearing a long dress! She felt as if she were ten years old, still a little girl dressing up in her mother's clothes. Her happiness bubbled inside her.

Suddenly the thought came to me, What will Randy say? He's so fiercely jealous. But he couldn't be jealous of Ben, the quiet studious one.

The music began. Doris turned to her escort, and put her left hand on his shoulder. Carefully he put his arm around her. He grinned shamefacedly.

"Haven't done much of this since those two years of dancing school. Remember? Mind if I count for a few steps?"

Her happiness was contagious. She loved to dance. After a few minutes he relaxed when he found that she followed his steps so easily.

"Having fun?" he asked.

She nodded, her blue eyes dancing in the light.

"Maybe it's not so exciting as dancing with Randy," I muttered to myself as I watched them, "but it is good— good!"

The music stopped and they swung hands as they walked back to find seats along the wall. Suddenly he held her hand up and looked at her ring finger. For a moment it seemed as if he would speak. But he turned his face away when her eyes fell.

A short, stocky senior claimed her for the next number, and the evening moved on.

With her other partners she chattered and laughed. With Randy she had always listened and laughed. With Ben she moved quietly to the music. He did not whirl, twist, try new steps, or jitterbug. He did not apologize. But he often looked down into her eyes with that quiet smile.

The dance was over with a confusion of good-nights. Ben brought her wrap and laid it on her shoulders. They moved with the crowd through the doors and into the cool night. Their hands touched and he held tightly to hers. He pressed the ring finger.

"I wish you didn't have to wear that ring anymore, Doris."

"Oh, Ben!" Her breath caught in her throat and she could say no more.

"I suppose I've no right to say anything, but I wish you were my girl. I've always wished it, but I couldn't get courage to tell you."

He stopped walking. "Want me to shut up? Have I made you mad?"

"No—no—"

They walked more slowly as they neared her gate.

"It was so much fun, Ben."

"For me, too, Doris."

"G'night, Doris."

"'Night, Ben."

But he stood by the closed door until the lights flared in her room upstairs, then moved down the street.

The next day in class my eyes searched for the ring on Doris' left hand. It was gone. She saw me looking and smiled. Then she looked over at Ben.

Courage

I learned his name that first day of class—Michael O'Kane. But he could never be called anything but Mickey. His short, curly black hair accented the clear, light color of his face. Eyes as dark as his hair danced with excitement or humor, or sobered to thoughtfulness or sentiment. His expression emanated eagerness, a sense of anticipation, and keen interest.

When I had organized the class and began to give assignments, his pencil flashed as he wrote in his notebook. Vital—that's the word I would use to describe him. I felt instant rapport with this boy who was so eager to live—to learn.

In assembly next morning, my eyes drifted over the students—pausing now and then as I recognized a face. Mickey was in the pep band, first clarinet. He was turning pages and arranging his music. Students around him asked the order of the pieces to be played, and he laid his instrument in his lap and turned to help them. His eyes danced as he took part in the repartee around him. I could not hear what was being said, but I could see him smile as he answered the jibes of his classmates, taking joy in the give and take.

The band director tapped the music stand with his baton, and each instrument was lifted into position. The downbeat, and the familiar opening of the school song brought us all to our feet.

By Friday I had read many placards on the walls calling for votes. Several attracted my attention.

> It'd be a shame
> If you'd not vote for O'Kane
> For Junior Class President.

> Don't be a stick;
> Vote for Mick,
> Junior Class President.

The following Monday I found a note from the principal telling me that I was to be sponsor of the junior class. At three forty-five in the afternoon all of the members of that class pushed and crowded into my classroom.

"Come on, Mickey. Let's get this over," someone called out. "You're still president from last year."

He looked at me, I nodded, and he came to stand near my desk. The students quieted when he began to speak.

"We're supposed to have our voting by ballots," he said, "but let's have official nominations. Doris, will you write the names of the candidates on the blackboard?"

Hands popped; voices called out a list of proposed names for president first. It was orderly confusion for a few minutes, then quieted to a buzz as Doris made the marks on the board to indicate the vote count. With the last ballot read and crumpled for the wastebasket, the students shouted, "Mickey for president!"

He ducked his head in response, called them all to silence, and asked for nominations for vice-president, for secretary-treasurer. The voting having been completed, Mickey made a few quick remarks about projects, and adjourned the meeting by saying, "Okay, Mrs. Doig, if we go down to the gym for a while? Will you go with us so we can have a little mixer? You play the piano, don't you? I can do a little swing on the clarinet, and the drummer is willing, I am sure."

About a week later Mickey came into my room after school. He stood at the door a moment.

"Busy, Mrs. Doig?"

"Not too busy, I hope," I said as I laid down a red pencil and lifted my eyes from English essays.

"You took a lot of German in college, didn't you?" he started.

"Yes, how did you know?"

"I asked the principal. He looked up your transcript. I want to learn German because I plan to study medicine. I want to be a surgeon. I can get a correspondence course from the university to learn the German, but I need some help with pronunciation. Will you give me a boost when I get stuck?"

I nodded and we made a tentative schedule of time for his coming in to work with me. Once a week after that we sounded umlauts and diphthongs, stressed accents, and tried to sound the roll of the German r. Often we talked of other things—Mickey of his ambitions, his love of music, his keen interest in all his subjects, and his enjoyment of sports—especially basketball. His slender fingers moved dexterously as he turned the pages of his German textbook. I thought of the future development in their skill as he continued in his training to be a surgeon.

On a crisp, sunny October morning I heard the news of Mickey's accident. Students were standing in little groups talking excitedly as I came down the hall. I caught snatches of their conversation and pieced together enough information to send me hurrying to the teachers' room to ask more.

"What's this I hear about Mickey's hand?" I said to Mrs. White, the instructor I found there.

"It's terrible! He cut it off in the meat grinder."

"What? A meat grinder! How come?"

"His dad's the butcher who owns the meat market. Mickey helps out after school and on Saturdays. Well, Mickey was making sausage with the electric grinder—lost almost all of his right hand."

Stunned, I walked out of the room and down the hall. His right hand! His piano playing, his fingers for clarinet, his grasp of the basketball, his ambition to be a surgeon—cut off in a moment of terrible horror!

My first class was junior English. For a few minutes of the period I let the students tell me about Mickey, explain to each other. Then with relief we turned to the prosaic study of Whittier and Holmes. With the ringing of the bell, the students filed out of the room decorously—too quiet—no pushing or shoving. Each student took Mickey's accident as a personal injury.

Mickey did not come to school that week. But by Friday I realized that he would be back soon and we must be prepared to help. When the junior class came in for English I tried to express my concern to his classmates.

"Listen, kids," I said. "Mickey will be back in school Monday. This is going to be hard for him. We've got to make it easier here if we can. For goodness sake, don't avoid him. Be as natural as you can, but don't just stare at him. He's going to need every one of you." There was hardly a sound in the room. I went on, "I guess that's enough of that little sermon," I finished abruptly, and we went on to our lesson.

It was a very pale-faced, quiet Mickey who sat in the front row of class Monday morning. He looked straight ahead, seeming to see nothing. I hesitated to direct a question at him. It was as if a sentence had been imposed on the whole class. The great white-bandaged thing lay quietly on the desk before Mickey. No one looked at it, only tried to avoid it.

Nothing I said seemed to reach the consciousness of any

member of the class. My words bounced off the walls and were lost. At the end of the period the class slowly left the room, the students avoiding one another's eyes, saying nothing.

We tried to be natural with Mickey, but he was completely withdrawn. Oh, he answered politely, absently, but he looked away as he spoke. When his eyes happened to meet mine, I saw a hurt in them as if something deep inside him was bruised and broken. I felt the pain, too.

He did not carry his clarinet case under his arm now as he went from class to the assembly room. He no longer appeared for the sessions of German study. When basketball season began, the other fellows hurried from the last class to be the first ones suited up for practice. Mickey quickly left the building after school, going straight home.

One night I stopped in at the meat market, hoping to talk with Mr. O'Kane. He was standing by the counter, idly strumming his fingers and staring out the windows.

"Mr. O'Kane," I said, "could I talk to you about Mickey?"

The tears began to roll down the man's face. He tried to voice a few words, turned his face away, tried again, then shook his head.

He moved some packages with his hands, then turned back to me.

"It's breakin' my heart," he said huskily. "Why didn't it happen to me? Why did I let him work with that old grinder?"

"You can't blame yourself," I said lamely. "He'll begin to have interest in his school again."

I tried to talk of his studies, of school, but I was not helping anything. I bought some meat and left.

Weeks later the bandages were taken off Mickey's hand.

Only a stump of the thumb and forefinger was left; the other fingers and the other half of the hand were gone. It was impossible for us to keep our eyes from resting on the maimed remains of his right hand. Mickey awkwardly used his left hand to make the almost illegible scratches for his writing, holding down the paper with the lobster-red, scarred stump.

Determinedly, he completed his assignments, unaccustomedly taking much longer than his classmates. He spoke little, but he was not sullen—just quiet, cowed.

In December the faculty went to the state teachers convention in Helena. One morning several of us decided to tour the cathedral. As we entered the nave and stood looking at the beautiful windows with stories told in colored glass, a young priest came to meet us. He spoke English with a soft Irish accent.

"Father O'Malley is me name," he said, "and would ye be wantin' a tour of the cathedral?"

He led us slowly along the south side of the great chapel, explaining the continuity of the pictures—first the lower ones, then the middle windows, and at last the small upper ones. I was walking close to him as we moved down the aisle and he asked me where I was teaching.

"At Three Forks. Are you acquainted with anyone there?"

"Oh, the lad—Mickey O'Kane. Do you know him?"

"Of course I do."

"Oh, the pity—the hurt—such a fine young man!"

We were near the altar. The priest stopped to explain the history of the building.

"This cathedral was built by the gold miners of Helena in the early days of Montana. These men were millionaires and spent much of their wealth on this building. The town took its name from the cathedral—Helena—instead of the original name of Last Chance Gulch."

As we were ready to leave the church the young priest moved near to me and said softly, "We're praying for Mickey often. Do ye the same."

Mickey's comeback was slow. Gradually he became less conscious of his maimed hand. Slowly his enthusiasm returned as did his smile for his comrades and his participation in class discussions, in school activities.

One evening after school as I sat at my desk correcting essays, I was aware of someone standing inside my classroom. I looked up, taking off my glasses and adjusting the vision of my tired eyes. It was Mickey.

"May I come in?" he said.

"Of course. I'm tired of these papers." I shoved them aside and waited for him to cross the room and drop into a student's desk near mine.

"Mrs. Doig, I want to go on with the German lessons," he said quietly.

"Good!" I said. "On Fridays again?"

"Yes, I think so. I want—I—" he stopped for a moment, then began again, this time with no tremor in his voice. "I've thought it out carefully. I've talked with Mother, Dad, and Father O'Shaunessy. I am still going to be a doctor. Oh, I know I can't be a surgeon. But I can be a general practitioner, or I can specialize in some field, such as psychiatry. For a few months I was so bitter I thought I would not go to college at all. I wouldn't even try to complete any of my plans. But I can't give up my dreams. I've got to be me. I'll just spend more time on study—on research—on learning."

He paused again. "But I need that German if I am going to do it. Will you help me?"

"You know I'll be glad to. Shall we begin this week?"

He nodded and smiled—the eager, Mickey-smile—and said good-bye. Each week we worked together. Then came graduation.

It was years before I saw him again after he had finished high school. I was teaching in a different school about thirty miles away.

One afternoon during my fifth hour of the day someone poked his head around the side of the doorway of my classroom.

"Got a free period?" he said.

"Yes, come in," I called out, then looked up. For a moment I did not recognize the young man who walked in. "Mickey, where did you come from?"

"From home," he said as he crossed the room with eager strides and held out his hand—the partial hand—for me to shake.

"What have you been doing?" I asked.

"You ought to know!" he said and laughed. "I have just completed my degree in medicine."

"Your doctor's?"

"That's right. Now for my internship!"

"Oh, I am so proud of you. I am so glad!"

"I was sure you would want to know. I knew you were teaching here, so I came to see you. Someone in the office said you had a free period so I hurried to find you."

If he hadn't been so tall, so mature and handsome I would have hugged him.

I Learn of Prejudice

During the school year of 1943-1944, emotions stirred deeply when we read of the atrocities of the war. We had been severely shocked by Pearl Harbor, our dignity wounded and our sympathy aroused by the infamous attack.

In the community where I taught there lived three Japanese families. For over twenty years the men had been regular employees of the railroad. Now we began to call them Japs, curled our lips in scorn, and looked askance at them. We became suspicious of their slanted eyes, their short stature, the pigment of their skin, and their broken speech which reminded us of our enemies.

Their children attended our schools and they must have felt the change in attitude from one of common acceptance to one of almost hostility. The members of the three families became isolated from community life.

On the first day of school in the fall, I noticed Niki Nipomo as I helped register students. Her actual first name was a long Japanese one, but everyone called her Niki. She was a beautiful girl. Her black hair was combed in a long bob, the curls touching her shoulders. She wore a bright red cotton dress with white collar and cuffs.

"You'll be in my senior English class," I said. "That'll be nice."

She looked directly at me, her black eyes searching for

any innuendo of derision. Then she answered my smile and said, "Yes, I like English. That's my favorite class, I think. But I like all my studies, even physics and chemistry."

I signed her registration slip and laid it in her outstretched hand. Her slender golden fingers closed over the paper and she moved on to make room for another student.

The following morning as I walked down the hall toward my room I passed two students who were talking vehemently.

"Darned little Jap," one said. "All because of her the advanced geometry class was changed to one o'clock in the afternoon. Sure upset my schedule."

"Yeah!" I heard the answer. "Why should she be given any special privileges? She's nothing but a Nipponese!"

My mind boiling with the insinuations of these words, I went into my classroom. Automatically I lowered the armful of papers onto the top of the teacher's desk, stooped to pull open a lower drawer into which I put a brown paper sack containing my lunch. I dropped into the swivel chair and sat with my elbows on the desk, chin propped on my hands, propounding the thoughts of bias that the students had expressed. This kind of thing could canker into turmoil.

Rising, I went back into the hall, down the front stairs, and into the principal's outer office. Through the open door of the inner office, I could see Mr. Ingerman's black curly hair, his bent head. Hearing me, he lifted his head.

"Want something, Mrs. Doig?" he said curtly.

"Yes," I answered slowly. "I'm sure there's a very good reason, but please may I know why geometry class time was changed yesterday?"

And I related to him the conversation I had heard.

"I just need to know," I continued, "so that I can face any criticism with the complete facts."

Mr. Ingerman's black eyes sparkled with fire.

"This animosity!" he said. "It is terrible in a peace-loving community."

He shook his head, then continued to speak. "Mrs. Nipomo is very ill—Niki's mother—tuberculosis of the lungs. Her husband is gone all day, working on the railroad. Because she is Japanese the state tuberculosis hospital refuses to admit her."

He paused a moment.

"The county nurse told me much of this," he explained. "Niki is taking all of the care of her mother. The nurse stops at the home once a week, in the morning, checks Mrs. Nipomo, explains to Niki exactly how to sterilize the dishes, the clothing, herself. It was the nurse that insisted Niki should complete her senior year in the high school. To do this she would have to take all her classes after ten o'clock in the morning. The mother sleeps much of the afternoon. I shifted the class schedule a little when I found out all this. It's the least I can do for the family."

"Thanks for telling me this," I said and hurried back up the stairs and to my room.

The first day of classes I had no opportunity to talk to the seniors without embarrassing Niki. She sat in the front row, against the west wall, aware of feelings of resentment about her, I am sure. She made no attempt to take part in the class discussion or to ask questions.

On Wednesday she did not come to class. As soon as the seniors had settled, I began.

"Listen, kids," I said earnestly, "I'm sure you would not want to be considered unjust or cruel, but those are the only words I can think of to label you. You are Americans—all of you—born here, with the rights and privileges promised you. Well, Niki Nipomo is an American too. She was born here in this town. This is her homeland. She has never considered herself an alien—why should she?"

For a moment I stopped and looked at the class. Then I went on to tell them what Niki was doing each day at home and why the class had been changed for her. Then abruptly I changed the subject. "Now open your texts to page seven. Let's read about Beowulf, the Anglo-Saxon hero of that epic. But first let me tell you about those Viking tribes that overran the island of Britain in the fifth century."

I turned to the blackboard and pointed to a crude map of England that I had sketched there the night before.

Niki was in class the next day, and we all—the students and I—pretended that nothing had happened. But I heard several girls ask about her mother and offer to explain the class discussion of the day before.

The school days passed by in an unbroken pattern. We were too busy most of the time to think of the war, but it was always with us, never very far from our conscious mind. The holidays approached. Traditionally the last day of school before Christmas vacation had been a gala experience.

"The teachers give the school assembly," the students informed me. "And it had better be good!"

"What do we do?" I asked.

"Oh, anything! Sing some songs for us. Read us a good story. Act out a little skit."

Mr. Ingerman appointed a committee to plan the assembly program.

Friday at two o'clock the bell rang two long rings and students poured into the gymnasium, shouting and laughing in anticipation. With more disorder than usual they shoved and pushed as they sat beside their pals in the folding chairs on the basketball floor before the stage at one end of the room.

Suddenly their attention was diverted by the squeaking sound of the opening curtain. On the floor of the stage sprawled the women of the faculty, lying in distorted poses, as if they had been dropped from great heights and had splattered onto the surface. Dressed in old slacks or faded men's overalls and work shirts, they lay still as if exhausted.

"The dance of the tired nymphs," the coach's voice announced in stentorian tones.

Slowly the music teacher raised her body enough to rest on one elbow, then slid back to her supine position. The language teacher lifted her torso from the middle up to a wishbone shape, then flopped again to the floor. The typing teacher brought her body to a half sitting position, rested there, a grotesque figure. Another instructor half stood, reached down to grab me by the top of my slacks. She lifted with a strong movement. My weight put too much of a strain on the top button of those old pants. With a "ping" the button popped off, flew across the stage and hit the heat register at the back. I grabbed for the top of my pants as she dropped me. Holding my slacks together, I rolled across the stage and out of sight of the laughing students. They howled and roared with glee. I did not see the rest of that dance.

The curtain was pulled and while the students applauded gustily, Mr. Ingerman quietly stepped through the opening in the curtains and stood waiting, a sheaf of white typing paper in his hands. The clapping stopped.

"A letter to Santa, from the faculty of the school," he announced. "Addressed to the North Pole, and sent by radio:

" 'Dear Santa, please bring our football squad some luck. That leg Ron Baker broke on the field is healing so slowly he can't begin to play center on the basketball team. Besides the cast limits his activities on the dance floor doing the Big Apple.

" 'To Eddie Leston bring a sense of direction. Next time maybe he won't try to make a touchdown for the opposing team. And that Sam Closson—he's left-handed in both of his feet. What can you do for him?

" 'Our girls need your attention, too. Susie Fanlon needs a new diamond on her left hand—any size stone—just so she can flash it in typing class. She gave the last one back to the owner a week ago and her hand is so unaccustomed to the loss of weight she can't type fast anymore.

" 'Angie Smith has starved herself so that she has to walk past twice to make a good shadow. Please bring her a ballast to keep the wind from blowing her away.' "

On and on he went with gossipy jibes. The students rocked with laughter.

" 'And don't forget the faculty. The English teacher wants a magnifying glass so she can read Glenn Jones's handwriting; the typing teacher should have a new pair of ear plugs; the science teacher a new rubber apron for the laboratory . . .' "

The letter hit the big ones and the little ones.

" 'And for me—please send a pair of brass knuckles to knock some sense into these poor students' heads. Respectfully, a tired principal.' "

After the holidays the tempo of the school bogged down in the becalmed days of January, picked up momentum with the basketball tournaments, and continued on at a high rate of interest in the plans for the spring prom.

In early May at the faculty meeting the principal read off the scholastic averages of the top-ranking seniors.

"Looks like Alice Graham will be top of the class and Niki Nipomo a close second," he concluded.

"Does that mean Niki will give the welcoming address at graduation?" the math teacher asked.

"If that Jap is allowed to give a speech of honor in our school, I am not coming," Mrs. Howard announced and slammed a book down on the desk before her.

No one spoke. The quiet was complete. No one even moved. I sneaked a look at the angry teacher. She was sitting stiff as a ramrod, her head tipped back, lips pressed tightly together, chin jutting out. An angry red covered her cheeks.

The coach twisted in his chair, then began to speak.

"Now, look here! Niki's earned the honor. She's a good student—you can tell by her grades. How can we deny her this?"

Mrs. Howard jerked her head. "Nevertheless, it is because of her people that our boys are dying on islands of the Pacific. Haven't you any feeling? Where's your national pride?"

"Have you told Niki of her rank?" one teacher interposed.

"Not yet," the principal answered, "but I will when the next grades are in."

"Well, I shall take this to the school board," Mrs. Howard said angrily. "They will back me."

The rest of us teachers squirmed in our seats, then began to mumble a support for the principal, a defense for Niki.

"Do you know the handicaps Niki has struggled against this year?" I offered placatingly.

"I know all I want to know," Mrs. Howard said quickly. "But I do know that four of our high school boys are going to have to go to the army right away without even being allowed to graduate. Whose fault is that, just tell me?"

The principal dismissed the meeting and we walked down the hall in little groups, talking excitedly. Mrs. Howard strode ahead, stopped at her room, and closed the door after her.

For a week the subject was mulled over daily in the

teachers' room. A few teachers hesitatingly joined Mrs. Howard in her crusade, but the others stood firm for Niki's rights.

Wisely, the principal did not call another faculty meeting. By the grapevine system we heard that Mrs. Howard attended the next session of the school board and vigorously protested Niki's being salutatorian at the graduation. They listened to her tirade, but evidently were not swayed in their decision to let the principal handle the affair with justice.

Graduation night, as senior sponsor, I was seated with the group on the stage. The music teacher played "Pomp and Circumstance" on the rented organ. I could hear the procession of the faculty and seniors entering the gymnasium. At a signal the coach pulled the curtain ropes and I looked out beyond the stage apron. I let my glance drift over the front rows—the faculty seats—and named each instructor in my mind. An empty seat caught my attention. "Mrs. Howard's chair," I said to myself. "So she kept her promise—or was it a threat?"

On out over the rows of seniors in dark red robes, I scanned the audience. Near the back I saw Mr. Nipomo's short erect figure. His eyes were turned toward his daughter on the stage beside me.

The organ finished the last notes of the march. Mr. Ingerman turned to Niki and nodded his head. She stood and walked to the podium.

"Mr. Ingerman, faculty of the school, fellow students, and friends," she said and began her speech of welcome.

A few weeks after graduation I heard that Mrs. Nipomo had died. A little later I learned that Niki had entered a school for nurses in a town two hundred miles away. Then in August a letter came to me from Niki.

Dear Mrs. Doig,

You'll be interested to know that I had no difficulty with my entrance test into this hospital. I have finished my probation and now wear a regular uniform with one blue ribbon stripe on my nurse's cap.

For the first time in several years I am accepted as a person of worth. Here, the students treat me as an equal. I am very happy with my work and my studies. I want to be a good nurse.

Sincerely,
Niki

I Learn New Customs

For the next two years I taught in a high school where I learned of many unfamiliar customs. Hundreds of miles from my native Montana, I adjusted very slowly to new ideas. Provincialisms in speech puzzled me. Instead of "up the valley" or "up the canyon or creek" it was "up the holler"; a short distance was "just a whoop and a holler" away. I learned that they "slopped the hogs" (we had fed the pigs in Montana) using a "bucket" instead of a "pail."

Often I heard the familiar "you-all."

"There is no such word," I reprimanded the students in English classes. "You can't use it."

"What do you say if there is more than one of you?"

"You say, 'You.' That is both the singular and the plural form of the word."

But before I was aware of it, I was saying "you-all" right along with the students.

One night after a basketball game I heard one small high school boy ask a big senior girl if he could "pack" her home. I waited around to see that! All he did was walk home with her. I was keenly disappointed.

Their speech was soft and slow, almost a drawl, while I machine-gunned my words, speaking with sharp pronunciations. One girl was always saying, "I 'spec." One day I said to her, "What do you mean by the word 'spec'? Do you mean *suspect, respect, expect, inspect,* or other words like that?"

"I don-no," she answered in her slow, soft speech. "I jus' mean *spec.*"

Their humor was another thing. My last name was Doig; another teacher's was Wolfe. On the blackboard in my classroom one morning I found this sentence: "We wonder when the Doig will bite the Wolfe."

Another morning they had punned in chalk, "You can't teach an old Doig new tricks."

The seniors chose me as their sponsor—not, as they carefully explained, that they liked me better than the other teachers, but their last year sponsor was no longer in the school and they didn't want to take the other classes' sponsors from them—a doubtful compliment. But we had fun that year.

In this class were twins—so identical that even with the experience of having twins of my own I had to study them very closely for days before I could identify Ronald and Donald. The commerce teacher could not tell them apart. It annoyed her immensely. They switched desks often, allowing the one who knew the questions to answer. She was vexed. One afternoon I sat beside her as we watched the intramural basketball games. The twins played on the senior team.

"Those two boys—the twins," she said, "they exasperate me. I can't tell them apart. They're always fooling me. Can you tell which one is Ronald?"

"I finally figured them out," I said. "Look! Donald's hair comes down to a point above his forehead. If he were a girl we'd call it a 'widow's peak.' Can you see that?"

Donald was facing us, dribbling the ball toward the basket. Stopping abruptly he tossed the ball through the ring and his class members cheered loudly.

"Yes, I do see that. Why didn't I notice?"

The next day Ronald passed me in the hall, turned about and faced me.

"Mrs. Doig, you must be the traitor!" he accused me.

"Of what am I guilty?"

"You betrayed us. Our commerce teacher knows Donald from me now, and you were the only teacher that could tell us apart. We had a good thing going for a while."

"I'm sorry. I didn't know you wanted it kept a secret. I have twins and they are disgusted when people can't tell them apart."

He told me what he and his twin had been doing. "Well, it's been fun while it lasted," he said, "but we'll forgive you."

He grinned and was on his way down the hall.

* * *

In late winter the class began to talk about a senior trip for spring.

"No use talking about it," one student said. "We'll never get it."

"Has it been a custom here?" I asked.

"Oh, yes, always," another senior explained, "until last year." He stopped there. No one said a thing. My face was a question mark.

"Haven't you heard?" the class president asked me gently.

"What?"

"What happened last spring?"

I shook my head, but I sensed the importance of what he was going to tell me by the quiet and awe in the classroom.

"Well, the seniors last year were practicing for their class play. At the dress rehearsal one of the fellows was goofing around with one of their props, a Civil War rifle. He leveled it off and said jokingly, 'Boom!' at the girl who played lead in the play, and pulled the trigger. With a terrible bang, the gun went off. When the smoke cleared away, everyone saw the girl lying on the stage dying, right there in front of them."

There was a moment of silence. Then I asked, "Did anyone know the rifle was loaded?"

"No! It hadn't been shot since war days—was just an old family heirloom that had been hanging over the fireplace for almost a hundred years."

"And the senior trip?"

"Canceled! Even graduation was more like a memorial service."

"But we're not to blame," someone said.

"Yeah, but my parents are scared for me to go on a senior trip for fear of what might happen."

"Mine too! I sounded them out just a few days ago."

"And if we can't have a senior trip there's no use putting on a play. That's given to raise money for expenses for the trip. So I suppose we won't even have a class play."

"Would your parents object to the play?"

"We can ask."

At the next class meeting the discussion was picked up where it had been left.

"My folks don't care if we put on a play," one student reported.

"It's okay to give a play if we don't have a gun in it."

"Let's do a farce," I suggested.

Someone sniggered. "What's that?"

"Oh, something you pour in your cereal bowl and put sugar and cream over," the smart aleck in the class joked.

"It's a comedy, isn't it?" one senior girl offered.

"Yes, a ridiculously funny, absurd play," I added. "I've been reading several plays. Here, some of you take one to read. Pick out the one you like."

I passed out the books.

"Bring them back Monday."

We decided to do *Charlie's Aunt,* and after tryouts began memorizing the lines. Night after night we went through the acts. Dress rehearsal was rough, but the boy playing Charlie's aunt carefully kept his falsetto during the entire part of the play in which he was impersonating an old lady.

Final night, the first act went smoothly. The audience warmed to the humor of the play, laughing at the right places. In the third act, Charlie came to me, where I stood behind the scenery.

"It's gone, Mrs. Doig," he said in agony.

"What's gone?"

"My falsetto! I can't make my voice get up there at all."

"You're just scared," I comforted. "Go out there and wow them."

I shoved him toward the right stage entrance. With his cue he walked on. His face contracted—no sound came from his throat at first. Then out came his natural, deep male tones.

Backstage we groaned in unison. The audience roared and stamped in glee. Chagrined we ground through the remainder of the play.

At the next class meeting the president asked the question: "What shall we do with the money we made from the play?"

"Let's go on that senior trip!"

"What will your parents say?" asked the class president.

"Well, we've hurdled this class play thing. Let's ask again."

"And not needle them," Donald said, "Just give good reasons why we should have this experience. Cook up good arguments—logical ones—all of you."

Another week passed. I waited, not wanting personally to

take the responsibility of sponsoring the seniors on this project, but interested in their happiness. They won—their parents talked to me individually and collectively, and finally capitulated.

Now the questions were where to go and how to travel.

"To the lake," they said in chorus.

World War II had just ended and we were still limited in many conveniences. Tires—new ones—were impossible to buy. Cars were old, and all trips had been cut down unless we could produce very good reasons for them.

"Let's each ask to take the family car," the smart aleck of the class suggested.

"But if our folks say no to the family car, then what?"

"Just keep asking—wear 'em down. That's what I do, and I always get what I want."

In the back of the room Ronald unfolded his long body from the class seat and stood up.

"That's not the way we do things in our family. Our car is old. The tires are almost worn out. We use the car only in an emergency, except to haul cream and eggs to town. I can't honestly tell them this trip is a necessity."

He sat down. The room was quiet. Even the smart aleck gave no retort to that.

"Why not try to get a school bus? The tires are good on all buses."

There was a murmur of assent.

"I'll ask about the bus," the president offered.

I put my two bits in then. "Say, let's take our food and cook in the cabins at the lake. The president can appoint a committee to decide what each one will bring."

Immediately after we had shed caps and gowns on baccalaureate night we met before the front door of the schoolhouse. Bags and boxes were piled high there. I could see jars of string beans and tomatoes, sacks of onions and potatoes, loaves of homemade bread, bags of spaghetti. The parents brought in the produce, then waited on the periphery of the group.

"Bring our kids back okay," they called to me as we loaded into the bus and whirled away in a cloud of dust.

My chest ached and my head was heavy as I felt the weight of responsibility of thirty lives to guard. "Bring our kids back okay" kept ringing in my consciousness. I could not sleep. If something should happen on this trip. . . .

All night we traveled, stopping at midnight for a snack. When daylight came, I could see the high hills near the lake where we would camp. In a few minutes I caught the flash of sun on blue water.

The students roused and began to chatter eagerly. They read off the names of the resort spots as we passed big signs.

"Our reservation is at Lazy Days, isn't it?" someone asked.

"Lazy D-A-Z-E?" a student queried facetiously.

"Maybe we've missed the turnoff," one boy suggested to Mr. Markin, the bus driver.

"We're almost there," he answered, undisturbed.

Heads were out of open windows, eyes looking forward and backward.

"First time you've been here, Mrs. Doig?" one senior asked.

"Yes—beautiful, isn't it?" I watched the curving inlets of the big blue lake, the jutting hills above the water.

The driver slowed the bus and turned sharply off the highway onto a graveled road. Dust puffed up and we partially closed the windows. For a mile or more we bumped along over the rough road. Another quick turn and we saw the big sign LAZY DAYS and then buildings beyond it.

"Two big cabins," I remarked. "East one for the boys and Mr. Markin; west one for the girls and me. Okay?"

We poured out of the bus and lugged our boxes and suitcases into our rooms.

"Breakfast in our cabin, in about thirty minutes," I sang out. "Then we'll swim and go boating."

About an hour of pancakes and fried eggs later, we met by the boat dock.

"Everyone in a boat wears a Mae West," the owner of the camp explained as he held bright orange life preservers.

"I can swim. I don't need that," one senior protested.

The man shook his head. "It's the rules," he said. "We'd lose our license if we didn't insist on this."

I grinned. "I promised to bring you back alive."

The student shrugged and slid the life preserver over his head. In two's and three's we scrambled into the big rowboats and pushed off onto the lake. I went with two girls who had never rowed a boat before.

"If you can't make it back, we'll come out and rescue you," one big senior offered.

"Hey!" I called out. "Just don't get too far out of sight for any length of time, will you? If I can see you once in a while, I'll not worry."

In the afternoon the smart aleck, with more spending money than the others, rented a motorboat.

"Anybody for a good fast ride?" he sang out.

Eagerly the boys responded, and the boat took off.

"Mr. Markin, how about going out in a rowboat with us?" another senior fellow said as he stepped into a boat.

"Nope! Can't swim. I don't trust those flimsy things."

"Aw, c'mon," the boy persuaded. "It's a great sport. And I can swim like a duck. If you turn the boat over, I'll save you."

The other fellow in the boat added his persuasions, and the bus driver hesitatingly allowed the Mae West to be pushed over his head. Cautiously, like a cat feeling out a damp spot, he reached one foot over the edge of the slightly rocking boat shaking his head and protesting volubly all the while. Good-naturedly the fellows joked with him as they helped him get settled on a seat.

"We'll teach you to row. You'll enjoy it."

As they pushed off I called, "Say, help me keep an eye on the locations of my students, will you? There's a couple around the cove to the right. I don't care if they're necking, but I don't want them to drown."

Out onto the center of the lake they rowed, their arms moving rhythmically with the oars. Suddenly the motorboat shot into sight, zoomed over toward the bus driver's boat, and then raced around and around it. The rowboat began to bounce up and down like a bobbing cork, with the waves caused by the motorboat splashing up against it. I could hear the loud voice of Mr. Markin who was clutching the side of the boat and swearing frantically. I waved my arms, yelled, and motioned graphically to the boy piloting the motorboat. After a minute or two he turned it away and went on down to the other end of the lake.

"That young fool!" I sputtered as I started back into the cabin to help the girls start supper.

Two days later, it was a suntanned, wind-burned group that climbed out of the bus before the schoolhouse door. Aloud I counted each one as he stepped onto the ground.

"I brought them back alive," I bragged proudly to the principal who stood there counting also, "as I promised."

He nodded and smiled.

Somehow, I felt the "jinx" on the school had been lifted. But one week later, I wasn't sure.

All spring we had been practicing for the music festival. Grade teachers had taught their students songs and dances. The boys chorus had worked on "Give me some men, who are stout-hearted men . . ." and other songs. A quartet of boys was planning a hill-billy sequence, with jugs and corncob pipes and faded overalls as props. For the girls I had chosen a short cantata.

"Let's all wear formals," one senior suggested. "We never get a chance to use our junior-senior banquet gowns more than once or twice."

"I don't have a formal," a sophomore said.

"I have two. Come borrow one of mine," the first girl offered.

The night of the program the gymnasium was filled with parents and friends. Nervously I flitted from backstage to the piano to check the order of the pages of music. Grade teachers marshaled their students to specified front rows.

The program moved forward smoothly, almost mechanically. After the hill-billy number which was performed on the front part of the stage apron, the curtain was pulled back to reveal the three rows of girls in long pastel dresses. A bit crowded for room, I stood close in front of them and raised my hand for the pianist to begin. The music flowed.

Even the second sopranos are on pitch, I thought to myself in surprise.

We were on the last number when one girl in the front row suddenly leaned forward and began to vomit noisily. For a second the girls around her stopped singing. Vigorously I shook my head and gesticulated my hands wildly. On to the end of the song we continued.

"Pull the curtain," I whispered hoarsely.

Yes, the jinx is still on, I thought as the janitor came with pail and mop, and I hurried to the washroom.

Jay

I heard Jay's raucous laugh before I entered the classroom. His loud "Haw! Haw! Haw!" sent a shiver through me—perhaps a sense of premonition.

When I began to call the roll, he laughed roughly at my pronunciation of names. I gave the assignment but before I could finish the last sentence he roared out, "You expect us to read all that guff before tomorrow! You'll be the one that's fooled." And again the loud "Haw! Haw! Haw!"

The next day when I called on him for an answer his loud retort was, "How do you expect me to know that? I'm not the teacher. You are. You answer it!"

Restlessly the students stirred, awaiting my response. With all the control I could muster, but probably with a sharp edge to my voice, I explained the simple answer.

Each day—and he was always there—his guffaws interrupted the class discussion. I sent him to the principal's office. He did not return until after the class had been dismissed. But the following day Jay was in class, disrupting as usual.

After school that evening I tried to talk to him alone. He smiled vacantly and said nothing. I went to the office of the principal.

"Oh, just try to get along with Jay," he said. "His father's on the school board, you know."

"School board or no school board, it's not fair for him to disrupt my class as he does," I said sharply and flounced out of the office.

I talked to his sister, trying to appeal to her for assistance.

"We cain't do nothing with him, Mizz Doig," she said. "Ma and Pa don't know what to do. They say he'll outgrow it some day."

"But he's a junior in high school. How did he get that far?"

"Teachers just pass him along, to get him out of the way I guess. Besides Pa's on the school board, you know."

The first test came. Jay wrote his name on the top of the page of paper, then drew foolish pictures across it. Not one word of answer to the questions. Indignant I handed it back with a scrawled F on the outside of the folded sheet of paper. With a great "Haw! Haw! Haw!" he held it high to show the other students of the class.

No matter how interested we were in a discussion, he would break in with his disturbing horselaugh. In the middle of a poem, while the students were listening with complete concentration, his stentorian "Haw! Haw! Haw!" would break the continuity and destroy the thought.

I asked the principal for permission to put Jay out of my class.

"Can't do that," he answered. "It would mean I'd lose my job."

Leaving the office, I muttered to myself a salty observation written by a famous writer, "The Lord made morons just for practice, and then he made school board members."

The unjustness of the sweeping generalization did not disturb me right then. My years of teaching had given me a great respect for school board members, citizens who would accept this thankless responsibility for a community. But right then I was frustrated, angry, baffled, and completely helpless.

A few weeks later I gave another test, this one over William Cullen Bryant. It was the last period of the day just after I had had a senior English class in which various students had given reports on Shakespeare. The blackboards were filled with lists of many facts that the students had given. The chalk writing had not been erased.

To this junior class I handed out the test pages. Instead of staring vacuously into space, Jay began to write on his paper. Unbelievingly, yet hopefully, I watched him scribbling away. It seemed incredible. A warm feeling of success crept through my consciousness.

I glanced around at the other members of the class. They were busily reading questions and writing answers. I turned back to Jay, observing him closely. He'd write a line, then look up at the blackboard. Again he would write something on his paper, then pause to look at the blackboard. I followed his gaze to the board.

The large script I recognized as my own hurried writing. At the head of the column I had written boldly "William Shakespeare." Curious, I again looked at Jay. The leer spreading across his face should have revealed something to me.

Carefully I scanned the items on the board. "Born in Stratford-on-Avon, 1632." The second item—written in a very good imitation of my scribbly handwriting—read, "The son of a country doctor, born 1794 in the Berkshire Hills." A third entry said, "Attended school where he learned a little of Latin and less of Greek." The following item was "Wrote most of the poem 'Thanatopsis' when only seventeen." The next note was "For forty-nine years he was editor of the New

York *Evening Post.*" Following this was the information "Married Anne Hathaway, several years his senior."

On down the information on the first blackboard face I read—the substitutions imitating my handwriting so skillfully, the erasures so cleverly executed. Grabbing an eraser I began furiously to wipe all the boards clean, then sank to my desk, completely disillusioned. The answers to the test on Bryant had been carefully interspersed with the facts on Shakespeare.

Jay laid down his pen, put his head on his desk, and slept during the remainder of the period. I was aware of the exchange of expressions of the other members of the class.

Completely at a loss as to what to do, I talked to other teachers.

"Oh, just give him a D minus and pass him along," they said easily. "You need your job, don't you?"

But I did not give up yet. I tried everything—offered to tutor him after school, tried to enlist the services of his sister, wrote notes home to his parents asking for their cooperation.

The year went by. His final grade—I recorded it myself in indelible ink—was an F.

The next year was a repeat of the junior year, as far as his schoolwork had been: no essays, no written assignments, nothing but blank pages for exams, and always that irritating "Haw! Haw! Haw!"

A week before finals the principal called me to his office.

"What are you doing about Jay's English grades?" he asked. "He needs them to graduate, you know."

"What can I do? They're all F's!"

"You could change them to D's."

"Maybe you could," I said quickly, "but I can't."

"You can't keep him from getting his diploma. It will be all your fault. You know what that would mean, don't you?"

"But I have no alternative. He's made an F in third year English and will have one in senior English. I would have no integrity if I gave him anything else. Besides it would not be fair to the other students if I did anything else."

"Oh, we could just erase the last year's F and . . ."

"But that's not fair!"

The principal gathered his papers as if to dismiss me.

"Well, you are on your own if you persist in this," he said curtly.

"You mean you won't back me? Won't stand behind me?"

"After all his father is on the school board," he said.

Numbly I walked out of the office. What could I do? I needed the job very much. I was the only support for my five small children. A black mark on my teaching record—a refusal to recommend me—what would it do to my future?

Perhaps foolishly—certainly indignantly—I stood by my decision. On graduation night, Jay marched across the stage, but was given a blank unsigned diploma. His parents refused to speak to me at all. I offered to make out a set of tests covering the courses, to leave them in the office. When he had completed them, I would come to the school, grade them, record a passing grade. I offered to tutor him. His mother and father turned away as if they had not heard.

The other faculty members ignored me as if I were a pariah, almost afraid to be seen talking with me.

Right then and there I lost all my sense of integrity—as far as school grades were concerned. I resolved never again to be the cause of a student's failure to graduate.

What should I have done? I don't know. But his failure still haunts my dreams and my memories.

Later in the summer an offer for me to teach senior English in my home state brought me back to Montana.

Jorrie

Absorbed though I was in teaching subject matter, I was also very much interested in the lives of my students. Each new class of young people brought a heterogeneous group of individual problems and interests. Some students were enjoyable from the beginning. Some I had to learn to love.

The first day of school was really just teachers' meetings and preparation. After most of the faculty had gone home, I sat at my desk looking through my pile of registration cards for senior English classes. Suddenly I groaned, "Oh, no! Not again!"

"Talking to yourself, Mrs. Doig?" The assistant principal put his head around the open door and grinned. "You know what that's a sign of."

"Yes, and you'd go crazy yourself if you had to put up with that boy another year."

"Let's see—could I venture a guess? You are talking about Jorrie Roberts?" Mr. Watson came into the room and telescoped his lanky body into a student's desk directly before me.

"Yes, I am." I scowled and shook my head. "I had him last year in junior English class. Two other teachers had kicked him out of their classes, and you gave him to me. Well, I put up with him and his nonsense for almost a year and I just—I just—" I sputtered.

"I know, I know. But Mrs. Doig, you're the only one who will take him. You seem to understand boys, especially troublesome ones. Jorrie wanted to take this English class—signed up for it himself even though he knew it wasn't required. When I asked him why, he muttered, 'She's the only teacher who likes me, I reckon.'"

"Just because I'm a pushover for the students," I said sourly.

"We don't want to expel him. That would put him on the streets and in the beer joints. Even if we can't teach him anything out of a book, let's try to keep him in school."

He jiggled his wristwatch a moment. "Have you looked at the record of his family?"

"Yes, I have." Some of my resentment was slipping away. "Nothing where the name of the father should be. Someone told me this summer that Jorrie's mother refuses to support him, doesn't want him around. He has a room somewhere and works at odd jobs during the school year."

Unfolding his long legs, Mr. Watson stood up. "You know why I am trying to keep him here one more year then. I can count on you, I'm sure. If anyone can get next to him, you can."

"Don't count on it—but I'll try." I picked up the registration cards and began to look through them again. The assistant principal went on down the hall.

School began next day with its usual clatter and confusion. Freshmen lost their way in the building, were sent to the wrong rooms by grinning seniors and juniors. Classes ground on to the last period of the day.

Before the last class, I steeled myself as for an attack. Here would be several of the most recalcitrant students. It would be murder to allow them to go to the study hall this hour of the day. Pity the study hall teacher! And here, of course, in this hour I would have Jorrie. I could hear his raucous laugh as he neared my door.

"Come on in, kids, and suffer awhile," I heard him say as he led the way into the room. My smile felt fixed, as if it had been painted on my face. As the class crowded into the back seats of the room, I glanced over the students and catalogued each one in my mind. Two of Jorrie's satellites were there too! That meant real trouble. There must be an easier way to earn a living than teaching, I thought. Well, I'll try to find some other kind of work next year.

The second week of school it was my turn to help chaperon the school youth center activity. Mr. Adams from social science came to help me. He sat at the downstairs door and admitted the students, checking ID cards. I watched the upstairs rooms. As the hours dragged on, the voices seemed noisier, especially those of several boys. One boy almost fell against me as he passed. His breath reeked with the smell of liquor.

"That's queer," I said to myself. "They're not allowed to go out of the building and come in again."

I began to watch one gang—Jorrie's—more closely. They kept going downstairs and coming up again later, each time noisier and more insolent. But students always milled around so much—I couldn't judge by that.

Midnight came, and my whole body sagged with weariness as I watched the last stragglers leave. I went down the stairs to the first floor and on down the hall. Suddenly I stopped. There were voices coming from the boys' washroom.

Turning, I called up the stairs, "Mr. Adams, you up there?"

"Be with you in a minute." His voice echoed in the empty corridors.

I stood still in the hall and listened. The sound of boys' talking died away, but no one had come out the door I was watching. The roar of a motor with twin pipes sounded distinctly from behind the school building.

Mr. Adams descended the stairs sedately, pushing his paunchy middle ahead of him.

"Everyone gone, Mrs. Doig? Doesn't the quiet seem good?"

"No, not all gone; there are boys in there yet." I nodded my head toward the boys' room.

Mr. Adams opened the door and stuck his head into the room.

"Empty," he called out, then went on, "Hey, what's this?"

The janitor, coming around the corner of the hall just then, answered him. "I think I can tell you what you want to know. Jorrie Roberts' car was parked just back of this room in the parking lot and . . ."

"What are all these bottles and cans doing here? And the windows are both open. Now what in the world . . ."

"I think Jorrie furnished the liquor for tonight—or his gang did—and it came in by way of the windows of this room. I shoulda' caught on sooner. If that kid don't beat all!" The janitor was muttering under his breath.

I just stood there shaking my head. Jorrie—those boys going up and down the stairs—why hadn't I guessed it? Yes, I could have him expelled. But what would I gain? I'll talk to him alone, I thought. And I went wearily on down the hall and let myself out the front door, so intense in my thinking I walked two blocks past my car before I realized it.

The talk with Jorrie next day produced no effects. There seemed to be no way to appeal to him. But I didn't like to accept defeat, and I tried every trick in the bag. Over the years I had built up some knowledge of boys. I had scolded them, censured them, cajoled them, forgiven them, and tried to understand them. But nothing I tried brought any good results from this boy.

One cold February afternoon Jorrie wasn't in class. I was concerned because he seldom missed school. He wouldn't miss the chance to torture me, I told myself.

"Where's Jorrie?" I asked one of his gang as the students filed out with the last bell.

"Dunno, unless he's sick."

"Would one of you boys look him up tonight?"

"Guess we could. Usually go to his room to play po—, I mean to his hangout every night."

I thought no more about it until the next afternoon when Jorrie's desk was empty again.

"Did you boys see Jorrie last night?" I asked after class.

"Yeah, he's sick, awful sick. We wanted to call a doc, but he cussed at us and said docs didn't know nothin'."

"Perhaps you should call his mother."

The boys looked at each other and shook their heads. "Naw, she don't care about him, won't do nothin' for him."

"Well, if he isn't better tonight, you fellows call Doctor Brunen. He's the county doctor and will come without pay. Will you do that? Don't even tell Jorrie."

They nodded briefly and hurried away. The next morning one of the gang slipped into my room before school.

"Jorrie's in the hospital. Double pneumonia, doctor said. Bawled us out for not callin' him sooner. That's gratitude for you," he said quickly and left.

All day long I thought of Jorrie. Being class sponsor, I felt a special responsibility for the seniors. Often we sent cards or gifts to members who were very ill. To each class of senior English I said, "Say, Jorrie Roberts is in the hospital with pneumonia. Can some of you go see him or send cards?"

The next day I managed to find time to go to the hospital after school. Jorrie's room had a big placard on it: "NO Visitors." I went home. But as the days went on his condition gradually improved. The senior class sent flowers. Then he developed a severe reaction to the drugs that had been given him. He was very sick. Blisters formed all over the inside of his mouth and down his throat.

The students had formed the habit of dropping in to visit him in the evening whenever he began to be allowed visitors. He was deluged with cards; some were handmade ones from the art department. As he began to convalesce, his room in the hospital became a meeting place for the high school students.

"Gotta go down and pep up Jorrie," they would say. Or, "Hey, been to see Jorrie lately? He can tell the funniest stories!"

Students who had never been friendly toward him, who had treated him as a stray mongrel, found time to visit him in the hospital.

I found a foolish toy, a Pluto dog that moved with strings, and a book about hot rods to take with me when I finally did go again to the hospital. I was amazed at Jorrie's sunken cheeks and colorless skin, but I liked what I could detect of the change in him. He had relaxed under all the attention. His hangdog expression, which had always been covered by a shell of bravado, had disappeared. He was still so weak he couldn't sit up, but he joked and laughed with the students as if he were one of their group.

Jorrie was out of school for six weeks. It was a long uphill grind, his return to health. His undernourished body was hard put to survive at all. One evening in March a sound at the classroom door caused me to lift my weary eyes from the essays I was correcting and turn them in the direction of the door. There stood Jorrie, as cocky as ever.

For a second or two the classroom atmosphere put the chip on his shoulder; then he shrugged and walked slowly across the room and leaned against the windowsill. His faded levi's hung loosely on his gaunt frame. His cheeks were hollow and pale, but his blue eyes smiled comradely at me as he hitched his belt tighter.

"For goodness' sake, Jorrie, how much did you lose?" I fussed over him.

"'Bout thirty pounds. But I'll pick it up fast, Doc says. Say, he's one swell guy. You know, I don't smoke anymore. Don't think I will again. Doc says my lungs'll be better off without it. Kinda hard on those beefy old lungs right now, I guess. I may even take his advice about hard booze, too. Bad for the ticker, Doc says."

He paused and looked out the window. "Say—uh—thanks for sending the kids to see me."

"I didn't have to *send* them, Jorrie. They came because they wanted to."

He turned and looked at me, then looked away. "I never knew how good it could make you feel to know somebody likes you. You feel kinda—oh—" He was gazing out the window again.

For several seconds the only sound in the room was the ticking of the big wall clock. I did not know what to say. At last I tried to answer him.

"Yes, Jorrie, I know how good it is to have friends—best thing in the world."

He turned and faced me. "And you'll never believe this, Mrs. Doig. My mother came to see me after I got pretty sick. Took me back with her when I got out of the hospital. I'm home now."

I Learn of Greatness

Perhaps I should explain why I had chosen to major in English when I completed my bachelor's degree. It goes back to the summer of 1928. I had to have additional college credits to keep up my teaching certificate. Besides, I was determined to graduate from college. So there I was at the university, carrying a full load of courses.

The summer was very hot. Sitting in non-air-conditioned rooms, with the temperature soaring each day, was real punishment. My clothes stuck to the chair seats, my arms were wet where they touched the desk tops, and I wiped the sweat from my face with a damp handkerchief.

The one o'clock class was a drowsy time. The food from lunch was being digested and contentedly I half dozed; I found it difficult to stay awake. The course was American novels. Mr. Mendel, the teacher, stood on a dais behind a lectern. His white hair waved back in even ripples from his high forehead. Rimless glasses slid down the ridge of his nose and he pushed them into place absentmindedly. He was tall, with broad shoulders and big hands—certainly not what I would have labeled the literary type. He stooped a little to read from the thick book on the speaker's stand.

"I think I'll begin with Hawthorne," he said that first day. "Call him a Puritan, call him a romantic or melodramatic; ridicule his complicated imagery if you like—but he could tell a story so well that a reader identifies with the characters and almost steps into their lives."

And he began to tell us about the *Scarlet Letter*. In a moment I was in the little New England harbor town, watching the great sail ships come moving majestically across the water to the quay.

It was incredible. In a few moments I had forgotten the hard seats, the unbearable heat, the overpowering urge to sleep. I was in the colonial town in Massachusetts walking with Hester Prynn, feeling her emotions of shame, humiliation, indignation, and love.

The loud ringing of the class bell for dismissal brought me back to the present. As I walked down the hall I pondered over the experience. Why had I been so completely carried away into a romantic world of make-believe?

The next day I rationalized my mesmerism in class the day before. I must have been so sleepy that I had just been carried away. I never really did like the study of English. Surely I would not let one teacher captivate my interests! But it happened again that day. This teacher had the ability to push aside the mundane world around me and lead me into a literary world of his choosing.

Was I the only one he had put under the spell? I looked around at the class members. No one scribbling in a book, no one nodding or looking aimlessly around the room. Instead each student gazed directly at Mendel as he read. The rapt expressions on the students' faces convinced me of their interest, and their absorption. I relaxed and allowed myself to be hypnotized by the tones of his voice, the sound of the words, but most of all by the deep involvement of his emotions and enthusiasm. I let myself enter another world—a living world of imagery, of adventure, of love, hate, and vivid action.

That summer I lived the literature of great writers author by author. When I stepped into the classroom, I walked out of the present into a land created by artists of the printed word, one which was more credible than the world in which I really lived.

Evenings I tried to analyze my shift of interest. Literature—all these writings coming alive—what a marvelous field of study! Why did I think so? Because of one teacher? What did he do? How did he do it? Why did I listen so eagerly? All summer I sought the answers. I resolved to try to do something of what this teacher had done! This I would attempt to achieve—this would be my goal—not just to imitate this man but to make literature come alive for my students.

During the next twenty years I nearly forgot that teacher, but I did not forget my ambition. Then one fall the state education convention was held at our high school. Sitting on the platform in the auditorium that first meeting was a row of distinguished men of education. The president of the organization introduced each one in order. He spoke of Mr. Mendel as an honored retiree. Carefully I looked at this educator. It must be the teacher I had had years ago.

After the meeting was over I searched the crowd for my former instructor. When the auditorium was almost empty I found him near the entrance doors.

"Mr. Mendel?" I asked.

"Yes." Behind those rimless glasses his eyes were as deeply thoughtful as I had remembered them.

"I am Elsie Doig, used to be Elsie Andes. Many summers ago I sat in a literature class you were teaching. Your presentation of the classics made me change my major in college studies. I became a teacher of English. Ever since then, I have tried to imitate your marvelous technique of teaching literature. I've tried to make the printed word become a real experience as I have read to high school students. You gave me an appreciation of literature that I have never lost. I just hope I have been able to pass on to my students a little of what you gave to me."

His eyes began to glow as if a light had been turned on inside him.

"All these years I have wanted to thank you," I finished lamely.

He took my hand and held it.

"I'm over seventy-five years old," he said. "What you have said is one of the most pleasing things I have ever had anyone tell me."

We talked of many things.

The next day, hurrying down the hall I was stopped by my principal, who held both arms outstretched, barring my progress.

"Whoa, there!" he said. "Wait, Mrs. Doig! Have you been enjoying the convention?"

Only waiting for me to nod, he continued, "Yesterday you made an old man very happy. I mean Mr. Mendel. He came to me and asked me if I had a Mrs. Doig in my faculty. When I said yes, he asked, 'Is she a good teacher?' Of course I had to say you were. Then he told me of your accolade for him yesterday. I've never seen anyone so completely over-joyed."

Bumblingly I stammered, "I was only trying . . ."

"Never mind—be on about your business." And he no longer stopped my progress down the hall.

I Learn About Failure

It is no fun being a failure. Hiding it helps one's ego, but a failure that is blatantly evident is difficult to face.

During a particular summer the assistant principal called me one day. "Elsie, have you ever taught a speech class?" he asked.

"Once—but with very little success. Why?"

"Well, you're elected. Mr. Benzer wants two journalism classes—a beginning class and an advanced one. That eliminates his hour for teaching speech. You're the only one I can call on. Besides, with Benzer taking the juniors that hour for journalism, you will have that period free. I'll give you one group the first semester and another entirely different group the second semester. So it will only involve one semester of preparation—elementary speech. You'll have a mixture of juniors and seniors in each class."

"Your word is law, I know. I'll try. May I come to the school and get a copy of the text I'll be using? You'll be there in the mornings each day, won't you?"

"Yep! I grind away each day except Saturdays."

He thanked me and hung up the receiver.

I really had no choice. It was like the Army: "Private Jones, you have just volunteered for . . ."

Before September I had read through the text. I wrote tentative plans for the semester. Then I discovered that my class was expected to put on a live radio program over the local radio station—fifteen minutes every other week. I read everything I could find about radio programming, visited the radio station, planned with the band instructor for records of the school songs, and read skits and shorts applicable for seasonable programs. I felt very inadequate but willing to learn.

Criticisms of our failures reached us quickly. Our interviews of the football men were stilted and unnatural. There was no humor. The students spoke too fast, didn't enunciate clearly. Unfortunately the fifteen-minute broadcast period occurred at two thirty in the afternoon so it was carried to every classroom in the high school by means of the intercom.

As a class we consulted. We practiced, scrounged around for humorous material that was not pure gossip, and tried to make our interviews more spontaneous-sounding. We found a few skits—really extended anecdotes—and practiced on sound effects. Really the only good thing about our program was the fading in of our school song, recorded by the band, at the beginning and end of the period.

But it was in November that I met my nemesis. A letter from the state speech organization informed me our school had been selected for the regional speech contest in December. Several dates were suggested. I was to choose one. An all-day Saturday program was projected.

The secretarial notifications to other schools would be taken care of by the organization, but I must arrange judges—adjudicators, they were called. I groaned and chose a Saturday as far in the future as possible.

Fortunately, I was acquainted with members of the speech department in the college right in our town. For final judges I could depend on them.

Immediately I began to enlist my students in entries: two for the extemporaneous, one for a dramatic reading—she decided to do the cut from St. Joan's White Armour speech—two for original, and on and on. Unfortunately I did not threaten to flunk any student who did not complete the contest. It's a horrible thought, but I wish I had!

In the gray hours before school began in the morning and after school until dark, I worked with individual contestants. Hour after hour we recited, taped, listened to the enunciation, gestured, emoted, and experimented with everything I knew—which wasn't much.

One by one the students dropped out—gave sleazy excuses, stopped coming. The Saturday of the contest approached. I had not one single entry. That last night—Friday—was eons long. Not once during the hours did I fall asleep. I rolled and tossed.

"What will I tell the other instructors? What will they say when they find out that I have no students in the contest? I can't face them. I wish I could be violently ill."

In anticipation I could see their accusing eyes. Cold chills went up and down my spine. Mental turmoil can be such terrible torture!

Before dawn I was dressed and ready to go to the school to check the final preparations for the influx of visitors. The registration table was set up with two of my students staffing that. The arrows were placed in the halls, and the huge placards on the doors of rooms where preliminary contests would be held. The student guides were at each strategic place in the halls. The stage crew had been alerted, and I knew I could trust them to follow instructions I had printed for them.

One by one we narrowed the list of finalists as the preliminary contests were completed. By afternoon the semifinalists were in the auditorium. Each time a speech teacher turned to me and said, "But where are your contestants?" I died a little; at least I felt that I bled inwardly. My face became a sickly green as I answered, "I have none."

It was worse than embarrassment—it was complete humiliation, an admission of abject failure.

The late contests were the most excruciating for me. Now even the judges—my friends from the college—were scanning lists, noting names of students and towns, asking me the same cruel question, "Where are your contestants?" My excuses were worn threadbare—half lies at best.

Ducking, hiding, and avoiding people, I finished the evening. It took great effort to stand at the door of the auditorium to say, "Good-night," to congratulate the right students, and to thank the individual instructors.

Exhausted, I drove home, walked the floor until I was almost dead, and then staggered to my bed.

I lay there and let the cold chills sweep over me, trying to blot out consciousness, until sleep took me into restless dreams. Even today I shudder to think of this horrible experience.

The Need to Have Someone Care

"Mrs. Doig," he said that day after class, "I'll be bringing the school texts for you to check in on Friday."

"Why, Harry? This is just February, not the end of the semester."

"Well, I won't be coming to school after that."

"I don't understand. Or, as you kids say, 'Snow again; I don't get the drift.'"

He grinned at the familiar expression, then turned away from me.

"Well," he began slowly, "you know my mother has married again."

"I think I heard that."

"This man—her new husband—is younger than Mom. It doesn't look so good, having a seventeen-year-old kid in her home. I sorta throw a monkey wrench into the works. She doesn't want me around anymore."

"Has she told you that?"

"Not exactly, but her husband was growling to her about 'feeding that big lout of a son of yours' the other day."

"And your own father?"

"Haven't seen him for years. He's never sent Mom anything for my support that I know. He wouldn't want me—I'd be like a stone around his neck. I sorta have to stay put to be in a school. He didn't want me in the first place. I heard him tell Mom that time 'n again."

"But what are you planning to do?"

"Try to get on as a cowhand at some ranch nearby. I heard that the Lazy-H outfit needs a cowpoke. Gotta get a job before spring when all the kids are looking for a place to work for the summer."

"Don't quit school yet, Harry. There are just three months to go until you have your diploma. Can't you find something around town here? Just an evening and Saturday job until May?"

"Dunno; haven't tried much, I guess. Pretty slim chance though."

"Would your mother object if you lived at home, if you weren't around much?"

He shrugged his shoulder.

"Promise me this, Harry. Don't quit school without letting me know about it first."

Reluctantly he gave his word. The next day, over a coke in the cafeteria, I talked to the guidance director.

"It's rough," he said. "I know a little about the boy's background. But these homes broken by divorce with second marriages baffle me. The youngsters have two strikes against them before they step up to bat."

"He gave me a promise," I explained. "Somehow I think what he needs more than anything else is to know that some person really cares what he does. Not that he was using me as a sounding board—I don't mean that I doubt his sincerity. But he needs to be given a sense of worth. If we could only help him. . . ."

"Encourage him all you can; keep him coming to school as long as possible. He doesn't realize how much a diploma may mean to him in the future. And keep me posted now and then," he said, and took his paper cup to the wastepaper can.

Friday I intentionally caught Harry's direct glance once as the students were settling in their seats. I lifted quizzical eyebrows. He shook his head and smiled. I grinned back.

Each day when the class filed into the room, I looked first to see if Harry occupied his desk. He was always there. Our glances often met. Friday I went to the back of the room during the last of the period to help students with a writing assignment. When the dismissal bell rang, I said in a low voice, "Can you stay a minute, Harry?"

He stood by his desk shuffling papers and books until the students were out of hearing distance.

"Did you get some work?" I asked.

"I'm washing dishes every night at the hotel," he said. "Not a glorified job, but it does give me three meals a day and a little spending money. It keeps me out of Mom's sight and that pimp she married. It's a far cry from punchin' cows—but it keeps my hands clean."

He laughed as he held them up for my scrutiny.

"Hard work," I admitted, "but nothing to be ashamed of."

He picked up his books and papers and went away.

Each week I managed to have a few words with him. The guidance man purposely "bumped into" him in the hall and casually asked about his work.

Week by week I checked off the calendar. The first week of May Harry came to see me during my free hour, his face beaming.

"Hey! Guess what! I went up to the Lazy-H Ranch Sunday," he said.

The expression on my face became doleful.

"Say, don't jump at conclusions. You know how you often warn us, 'Don't get your mental exercise jumping at conclusions!' Well, anyway, the foreman there promised to hold a place for me until after graduation is over. How's that for a great piece of news?"

"Best thing I've heard for weeks," I said.

"So, I'll try not to break any more crockery at the hotel until after the middle of May."

"I knew you could do it," I said proudly, afraid to embarrass him by saying more.

The night of graduation I sat there listening to names being called, watching students in long gray gowns swish across the stage to receive their diplomas and shake hands with the principal. I glowed with joy as the name of Harry Beechman was read off. The long-legged student strode out of the wings, his gown swinging, and crossed the stage to accept the coveted document of graduation. It was more than a symbol of learning; it was a badge of courage, of determination, and of honor.

I Learn of Poverty of the Rich

To myself I called her my "poor little rich girl." Her father was a very wealthy man, I knew. But I was interested in Judith as a person. Of course, my principal contact was in English class. She wrote well, expressing herself concisely in very mature concepts. Her style was almost journalistic.

She wore simple clothes, deliberately conforming to the sweater-skirt pattern of her associates. But the wool of her pleated skirts was fine French material or Italian import and her sweaters were of delicate Angora with intricate knitted patterns. She spoke familiarly of Athens, London, Rome, and the little room where Keats lived close by the Spanish steppes.

With her classmates she seemed at ease, but distant. She seldom engaged in the popular badinage. There was no arrogance; it was more like the tolerance of an older, wiser adult.

One day I asked her about this.

"I don't know," she said, "unless it could be that I feel older than the other students. They seem so immature."

"How old are you?"

She grinned. "Seventeen," she said and waited a moment. "But for two summers now I have managed a store for my father during the whole season—just for kicks. This included the personnel, the buying—everything. He dropped in once a

111

week, but he gave me free rein. He's always expected me to think as an adult."

For several weeks I did not talk with her alone. The A she earned for a grade each quarter satisfied what I required of her. Sometime in November Judith stopped at my desk at the end of the class period. After the other students had poured out of the room, she turned to me.

"I won't be here for class tomorrow," she said. "I'm going to Butte tomorrow to see an oculist."

"You're having trouble with your eyes?"

"Not really, but I get dizzy sometimes and then my vision is not clear. It must be that I need glasses."

"Will your mother go with you? That's two hundred miles of driving."

"No. I haven't even told her. Besides she's too busy with her social things, and I don't want to bother her. It may not be anything but my imagination."

She was in class again Friday. Again she stayed in her seat at the back of the room until the students had all gone, then came slowly to stand beside the lectern where I was sorting and putting away notes. I looked up at her, expectantly.

"Reporting!" she said curtly, unemotionally.

I smiled. "I am glad to see you back," I countered. "What did the oculist say?"

"The specialist examined my eyes carefully," she explained. "He said they were perfect, with twenty-twenty vision. But he suggested I go to our family doctor for a complete checkup."

"Which you did?"

She smiled ruefully. "Appointment for tomorrow at ten." Involuntarily she shuddered. "How I hate to have them put their cotton-pickin' hands on me, to have them touch me!"

"And that dizziness?"

"Still with me."

"Did you notice it when driving up over the continental divide to Butte in that high altitude?"

"No more than here at home. But it blurs things now and then."

She shifted her books in her arms. "Oh, it's really not anything—probably I'm becoming paranoid."

She shook her head as if to shake away the thoughts in her mind—or to clear her vision.

"See you Monday," I said.

She waved from the doorway and smiled. It was Tuesday, however, before I saw Judith again. With difficulty I avoided gazing at her during the class period. Afterward she came to my desk.

"And what did the doctor decide?" I asked quickly when the room had emptied itself of its students.

"Malnutrition!" she grimaced. "Imagine my letting myself into such a foolish mess! How juvenile!"

"But why, Judith?"

"I'm not sure. The doctor grilled me for an hour, asking every imaginable question. For two days I have been catechizing myself. I've concluded that I just don't eat enough—mostly because I eat alone and it's not interesting."

"But your mother . . .?"

"She is always gone to a social something or other. She eats irregularly and is always on a severe diet at home. In the mornings I never see her because she's still asleep. So I eat alone—or don't eat. I drive home at noon, but she's not there. She's usually gone to play golf or for a fitting for a new gown. I grab a bite to eat and come back to school. In the evening Mother's attending a bridge party or getting home late from one and does not want to eat."

"Your father, too?"

"He's twenty years older than my mother—a business-man. He owns and manages many stores. He keeps a business residence in St. Paul, another in New York, and flies to Europe now and then or to South America. He's seldom at home, but when he is, he's on the phone or in his study working. I try not to bother him.

"I study or read and when I get hungry I go to the kitchen. But when I've put together a snack and I sit down at the table, I can't eat so I toss it into the garbage can."

"Do you get plenty of sleep?"

"That's another thing that I do that I know better than to do. I stay up very late—I don't like to go to bed when it is so lonely in the house with no one but me there."

"Have you talked to your parents about all this?"

"No!" she said emphatically and turned away. "And I'm not telling you this to get sympathy. But you asked. . . ."

"I really wanted to know. I care about my students; you know that."

"The doctor says that if I don't improve my physical condition he must talk to my father. He laid down definite specifications about the quantity and quality of my meals. Oh, he makes sense. I'm wolfing down milk and eggs and vitamins."

I could feel her impatience, her anger with herself and the whole situation, and her distaste of the subject, so I said, "I'll be looking for some color in your cheeks soon, and not artificial painted-on color."

She nodded and was gone.

I watched her in class and waited for her to open the subject again. Weeks later she stopped to talk to me.

"My pink cheeks give you the answer you've been wanting to know?" she asked teasingly.

"I hope so. What does the doctor say?"

"Still scolds, but not so threateningly."

"And your parents?"

"Still unsuspecting." She gave a twisted smile. "Or should I say not noticing?"

The next June Judith was driving home in her new Cadillac with a college boy one night very late and went off the approach of a river bridge and into very deep water. The bodies were found the next day.

Even today when I think about it I am haunted by the incident. Could I have helped this "poor rich girl" in some way and perhaps saved her life? Who failed? All of us, I concluded.

I Learn from a Student
of the Orient

I had been teaching in this college town for six years. In the summers I often picked up courses to earn credits toward a master's degree.

Then I married Wendell Townsend, a cowboy-rancher friend I had known for many years. Wendell was now in the sheet-metal business. I continued to teach. My husband had a house built for us near the college campus.

That fall I was back in the classroom as usual. It was the first Saturday in September that the telephone rang while I was mixing bread in the kitchen.

"Mother, telephone!" a daughter called.

Gingerly taking the receiver with floury hands, I held it to my ear.

"Hello!"

"Mrs. Townsend?"

"Yes."

"This is Mr. A—— in college housing. I know your home is very near the campus. We have no room left in the men's dorms this fall. Would you be able to take a foreign student for the college year?"

"Uh—uh—uh!" I made inane monosyllables as my mind raced.

"Do you have any room you could make available?"

"Well, perhaps—let's see now. My oldest daughter left for college a few days ago. Yes, I suppose—."

"This fellow we want to put in your home will need a room and breakfast privilege. He can eat the other meals at the student union. His name is Mirza Heider Beg. He comes from Pakistan and has had two years' study in the university at Karachi. May I have someone bring him to your house? Would this morning be convenient for you? Say, ten o'clock?"

"Yes, I guess so."

"Thank you, Mrs. Townsend."

I turned back to the bread, put the dough in a bowl, and covered it with waxed paper.

"Come and help me," I called out to my daughters. "We have to clean Beverly's room for a college student."

Promptly on time he arrived, a small slender fellow with shiny black hair combed smoothly back from his forehead and expressive black eyes. He stood by while the driver of the car unloaded several large pieces of luggage and drove away.

"I am Mirza Heider Beg," he said in carefully articulated British speech.

We shook hands. I led him through the garage and down the stairs leading to the recreation room and the bedrooms adjoining.

"This will be your room," I said. "Here are closets, a built-in wardrobe and drawers," I opened doors and pointed.

"This is the bathroom; here are the towels and washcloths. You'll share this with my nephew who is staying in this next bedroom and attending the college."

We went back up the stairs.

"You can go out this way through the garage. That will always give you an entrance. We never lock the house or the garage, so you'll not need a key."

I left him to carry his belongings to his room. From my windows in the kitchen I watched him. He stood for a few moments looking at his pieces of luggage, then began to lift them. He seemed unaccustomed to the task of taking his bags to his room, but I did not offer to help.

Later he tapped at the kitchen door and entered the room.

"Is there no one to draw my bath?" he asked.

"No, I'm afraid you'll have to do that for yourself." I smiled. "We all wait on ourselves here."

"Thank you," he said softly and went back down the stairs.

I heard the water running for a very long time. Later as I began to wash the dishes I found no hot water. All gone! I couldn't believe it! That forty-gallon hot water tank emptied!

Later I heard the back door shut gently and knew he was leaving, probably to get his lunch at the college.

In the afternoon when he returned I explained the kitchen facilities, showed him where the cereals and coffee were kept, and pointed out the refrigerator and its contents.

"We eat breakfast very early in the morning," I said. "What time do you usually get up?"

"I rise at eight or nine."

"And your first class?"

"At ten o'clock."

"We'll all be gone when you get up. I'll make an extra amount of coffee for you and leave it here in the percolator. Just put the plug in here when you're ready. Then be sure to turn it off when you're through."

I showed him how to do it, and how to use the toaster. He thanked me and returned to his room. The odors of strange-smelling tobacco drifted up from the basement along with the soft strains of oriental music.

We saw Mirza often. When I came from school in the afternoon he was usually curled up in one corner of a davenport, books on his lap. My children taught him to play croquet. He enjoyed archery with them on the back lawn where the target was propped against a tree. With fascination he watched one daughter who was a majorette practice twirling and throwing her baton.

He came to me one October evening as I sat correcting English papers.

"This mathemateek!" He accented the last syllable. "On my papers the instructors put always a red F. I do not understand what to do. Could you help me, please?"

He held the opened book toward me and pointed to a page. I shoved my work aside and looked at his book.

"Algebra," I said. "Did you study this in your university in Pakistan?"

"Only a little. The instructor here goes so very quickly."

"Let's see—you're in engineering, aren't you? Then you must learn this to be able to get your degree. Well, let's have at it!"

"Beg pardon!"

"Oh, that's a Western expression, a colloquialism. It means let's try to do it."

For an hour or more I explained how to solve algebraic equations. At last he closed his book and leaned back in the chair.

"Mirza," I said, "you are accustomed to the warm climate of your own country. Why did you choose to come to a college in Montana where it is often very cold?"

"You see the color of my skin," he said unabashed. "It is darker than yours. If I had entered a college in your southern states I would have been insulted. I would have been denied many privileges. Many people would have shunned me."

119

"You are so right," I said. "And we are not proud of the situation. Now, tell me about your people. Do they live in Pakistan?"

His eyes lit up and he smiled. He had "talking" eyes.

"No, in India."

"But you come here from Pakistan?"

"I chose to go to Karachi for an education. My people because of their religion remain in India."

"Do you have brothers or sisters?"

He nodded.

"Tell me of them."

For a long time he talked, his soft voice, his rhythmical tones pleasing to the ear.

"Mirza, do you still have the caste system in India?"

"In some places, away from the seacoasts, but not much in the cities. We are becoming westernized. Many changes we have made."

"But why do you still have castes?"

His eyes flashed and his body became rigid.

"Here in your country you have a terrible caste system," he said. "Because of the color of people's skin you put them in lower classes and treat them with disdain."

"Yes, we do," I said. "And I am sure we have many changes to make, too."

His body relaxed, he picked up his book, and stood up.

"Thank you very much," he said in his correct British accent, and bowed slightly from the hips.

"I'll be glad to help you again when you have difficulty." Wearily I pulled my papers back and put on my glasses.

In December I began to plan to teach the writings of Kipling in my English literature classes. An idea came to me.

"Mirza," I said one Saturday morning, "would you do something for me?"

"Yes, madam," he answered without question.

"I have four classes in which we are studying Kipling's stories and poems. We would have a greater appreciation and understanding if you would come to tell us about India. Do you think you could get excused from your college classes to do that?"

"I let you know," he said. "What day?"

"Tuesday or Wednesday would be best for me."

"I tell you Monday night," he promised.

The following Wednesday Mirza rose early and took his bath. He ate breakfast with us. He was wearing his richly embroidered silk lounging robe.

"Can you wear your native clothes?" I asked. I had seen him in these once.

"If you wish," he answered simply.

He went to his room and returned later dressed in close fitting white pants and a long black coat.

"This is what you would like me to wear?" he asked.

"Oh, yes. And now, do you have any native things you brought from India that you could take to show the students?"

He nodded and brought an armful which he took to the car. We drove to my school. When the first class began, I introduced Mirza and encouraged him to talk to the students and to tell about his homeland. They listened quietly. After a few minutes he seemed at a loss what to say.

"Do you students have questions about India? For instance, would you like to know about the courtship customs there? The marriage rites and ceremonies?"

Mirza began again. Later he played a recording of native Indian songs, translating the words for us, explaining their meaning.

"This one tells of a little white cloud. Here in Montana

you talk of the beautiful sun. In my country where it is often very hot, we are so very grateful for shade and for the little white clouds that give us coolness."

We listened to the music, noting the weird woodwind sounds that seemed so mournful, so plaintive, then so light and happy. The strange instruments produced unusual chords and half tones.

Class by class his lecturing improved. At noon I took him to the cafeteria to eat lunch with me there. Sitting at the faculty table, I introduced him to other teachers.

"This spaghetti has beef in it, Mirza," I warned. "If you do not eat meat—"

"I am Western in my eating," he interrupted. "I like American food."

After classes were over I took him home. As we drove into the garage, I put a ten-dollar bill in his hand.

"No, no," he protested.

"Yes, yes," I insisted. "You earned that." And I thanked him sincerely.

When I came home from school the next day I found on the dining table a dozen gorgeous red roses and a card beside them inscribed with the one word, "Mirza."

One afternoon during the Christmas vacation Mirza came to me in the living room.

"Please, Mrs. Townsend, there are some hungry students in the college. The student union is closed for two days. These students are from distant countries, from Israel, Lebanon, and Iraq. They have no place to go to eat unless they walk down to the town. If I be allowed to cook for them a meal this afternoon—yes?"

"Yes, of course," I said.

He thanked me and hurried outside. In less than an hour he returned with his arms filled with grocery sacks and followed by five young fellows. Eagerly they crowded into the kitchen.

"May I watch?" I asked.

"You are welcome," Mirza answered.

From the brown paper bags he took two dressed hens, vegetables, small boxes of marjoram, turmeric, and other seasonings. Now and then I peeked into the room, but mostly I tested the aromas coming from the kitchen and tried to identify them. I listened to the combinations of languages being spoken, understanding nothing but the joy of comradery in their voices.

Following the clatter of dishes being washed and the diminishing sound of voices and feet on the stairs, the strong smell of oriental tobacco indicated Mirza was entertaining his guests in his room.

In the summer he moved to a fraternity house. We missed him, but it was good to have hot water for the laundry on Saturday morning.

The following year he came to tell us good-bye.

"You're going home, Mirza?"

"Yes, to my people. I keep my promise."

"Does this mean you'll be living in Pakistan?"

"No, in India. I have learned many things. Now I return to teach others."

He shook hands with each of us, bowed formally, and was gone.

I Witness Growth

Jack was noisy and handsome. He was tall with dark, curly hair and even features—a modern Adonis. The high school girls adored him. He absorbed their adulation as if it were merely deserved. He exuded charm and superego, laughing and conversing easily with the fellows. On the basketball floor he excelled, often sinking the greatest number of baskets during a game.

I knew his parents—his father a professor at the college, his mother interested in voluntary social work in the community. I had had his older brother in English class the year before. He hadn't worked and wouldn't study—just kept a seat warm. One Monday he and a senior girl came to class early.

"We thought you would like to know Shirley's change of name. She and I were married over the weekend," he said.

"Oh, when did you decide to do that?" I asked.

"We found out that we both liked the same kind of beer and both smoked the same brand of cigarettes, so we decided that we were in love."

Their marriage lasted just six months.

But Jack was not like his brother. He enjoyed the class situation, if only to criticize school. He ridiculed the education system, especially the English instruction. He was a verbal young fellow, talking easily and at length on many subjects.

"We've had this same stuff again and again," he derided when we studied rhetoric. "Why can't we get on to something new? What relevance does all this junk have to our lives?"

When we got into literature he quieted down.

"That Chaucer guy—he could really describe those characters. But I like the gory tale of Beowulf better. Now, that's the kind of story I would write."

"Try writing one," I said.

His first essay made me furious; each sentence was loaded with profane words. But the idea was clever—a pseudo-scientific fantasy. I crossed out swear words, inserted expressions of vivid imagery, and explained in the margins.

When I handed back the students' writing I watched the play of emotions on Jack's face. There was anger and chagrin. After class he stopped by my desk.

"What's this criticism for my choice of words?" he asked curtly. "I'm just being realistic. That's the way we express ourselves today."

"Jack, an excessive use of any word is usually useless repetition. Unless it is a key word or one used for emphasis or continuity, it shows lack of originality and a limited vocabulary. There's no point in careless repetition. Search for new words, original expressions, phrases that have more power," I explained.

"Do you mean to tell me that we never use swear words in writing?"

"No. But you don't use them just to shock the reader. In dialogue you might want realism. But you're not putting across any new ideas or any original concepts by the constant splattering of profanity through your writing as you have done. You're capable of better work. I think you have a germ of genius, a spark of creative ability. Use it effectively."

He walked away. A week later he came into my room early in the morning before classes convened.

"Got a minute, Mrs. Townsend?" he said.

"Just about that!" I said, looking at my watch.

"In the middle of the night this story idea came to me. I took a flashlight, got down under the covers of my bed, and wrote it. It was almost morning before I finished. Will you read it and comment?"

"Be glad to, Jack."

He handed me the pages of manuscript filled with his handwriting. That night I read and reread his story—another wild, fanciful tale filled with melodrama and exciting adventure. But there was a certain fascination in the unreal plot and I wrote commendations on the paper. Jack was pleased when I gave it back to him.

"Save it," I said, "and work it over now and then."

Not long after that his mother came to see me at school.

"I can't understand my son Jack," she said, laughing. "Suddenly he's begun to study. When I ask him what he's doing, he says, 'English.' What great assignments you must be giving! Not that I'm complaining. It's a welcome change from his life of carousing around with his old cronies."

I told her a little of his writing.

Often Jack brought me an extra writing—sometimes an essay satirizing some modern custom or event, sometimes another short story. He wrote of hunting, of huge monsters, or of bloodcurdling events.

"I'm even interested in my speech class now," he told me. "It gives me another 'out' for my ideas."

After his graduation I did not see him again for several years. I heard he was attending the university miles away from home. One summer I was driving through a very small town in Montana on a national highway. It was about three o'clock in the morning. The town was very quiet, not a moving car in sight. I had been barreling along at sixty-five miles an hour. At the outskirts of this town I ignored the huge "slow down" sign, then deigned to reduce my speed a little when I saw the speed limit of twenty-five miles an hour. I met no one as I drove through the silent town on the main street.

I had reached the other side of the town when I heard the piercing wail of a police siren. Impatiently I pulled over to the curb, muttering under my breath something about "Nothing but a wide place in the road."

A highway patrol car pulled up beside me. The officer got out—his flashlight glaring through the car window.

"Let me see your driver's license, please," he said crisply.

Rummaging through my purse I found my billfold, flipped it open, and held it out the window. The patrolman focused his light on the printing for a moment, then stuck his head into the open car window.

"Lady," he said severely, handing out each word of judgment, "you were driving forty-five miles an hour in a twenty-five-mile speed zone." He paused suddenly as he flashed the light in my face, then said in a tone of glad surprise, "Mrs. Townsend, what are you doing here?"

Embarrassed, I stumbled over words. Then, beginning to think, I said, "Jack, what are you doing here? What about your studies at the university? Have you given them up?"

"Nope," he said as he leaned on the door and relaxed. "I'm studying law there. It's great! But summers I work at this to earn money for my college expenses. Besides I get a worthwhile experience in this, learn a lot. I will graduate next spring. How's that for a surprise?"

"It's a good one," I said firmly. "Have you kept up with your writing?"

"Not enough time right now. Once in a while I make up stories as I drive along. Mostly I live stories that are as dramatic as the ones I used to make up. I'm saving them up for some later day."

"You should have a great number of tales you can tell—real ones."

He gave me back my driver's license, but did not take out his little book.

"Aren't you going to give me a ticket?" I asked.

"No, I was just going to jaw you out a bit. Don't even feel like doing that now. I'm so glad for the chance to talk to you. Besides, you got me out of a few scrapes a few years ago and gave me a push in the right direction when I really needed it."

"I'm glad, Jack," I said.

We talked awhile in the late hours in that quiet town, about his mother and father, his brother, his studies, and his ambitions.

"Some day I may need a lawyer. If I want a good one, I'll know whom to call. Good luck, Jack!"

He waved as I drove away.

Another Kind of Communication

My husband's job took him to a large city in the midwest. At the end of the school year we moved with our family to the suburbs of that city. Urban life was a new experience for us.

For one year I worked as a proofreader in a publishing house. But this was not for me. I missed the students and the classroom situation.

In the fall I began teaching English at a high school on the rural edge of the suburb where I lived. Many of the students lived on the farms nearby. Slowly I absorbed the culture of the urban-rural combination. TV was the steady diet. I learned to use examples from the "boob tube" to illustrate a point.

In this school discipline was extremely lax. The principal was gentle and wanted to be a "good Joe" with the students. There was no use sending a refractory boy to the office. He would just return to the classroom grinning, swagger to his seat, and leer at the other members in the class knowingly. "An easy victory" was signaled with the two uplifted fingers.

One day near the end of the school year, the principal called me into the office after school.

"Mrs. Townsend, how many graduate credits have you on your record?" he asked.

"I don't know exactly," I answered. "Why?"

"Would you like to be a counselor? We must have a full-time counselor next fall. The students come to you for counsel all the time. You might just as well be paid for it. Are you interested?"

"I haven't finished my master's degree yet."

"How much more do you need for it?"

"At least another summer of residence work I am sure."

"We could increase your contract by a thousand dollars for next year. Would that help?"

"I would want to go back to Montana State University since I have most of my graduate work from there. And of course I would have to talk to my family. I'll talk to them."

We had a family caucus that weekend. Beverly, the oldest daughter, was a mathematician at the White Sands Missile Range so she was not at home. The oldest twins were graduating in June, one from the University in Colorado and one from the school of nursing nearby. The youngest twins were seniors in high school that year.

"Why not?" they said.

"I'll stay home this summer and keep things running," offered one of the oldest twins.

"I'll be at the hospital here in the city and home often," said the other one.

"If that's what you want," my husband said.

Before school was out in May, I was enrolled in college and had made application for my master's degree. My husband and the younger twins drove me out to Montana and stayed until I was settled in a room near the campus of the university.

My classes were early in the morning. Afternoons I studied in the library. Evenings and late into the night I pored over texts, wrote research papers, and took notes. Most of the time I was too busy to be lonely for my family. On the

Fourth of July my husband and son drove all the way to Montana to be with me during the weekend holiday.

The work was hard. I was completing my master's in English as well as counseling.

In my field before I was finally accepted as a candidate for graduation, I had to pass an oral examination before a board of faculty members from the departments in which I had studied and answer any questions that these dignitaries might ask me. A date was set for this examination; the members were chosen to do the questioning. The time drew near, and I began to be afraid.

I reviewed from old textbooks, studied rules, and accumulated facts. It had been many years since I had begun college. I had forgotten so much of what I was supposed to know. How could I answer questions about the history of education, about the new school laws of the state, about—oh, any number of things? I was filled with worry.

"They're toughening up on the graduate school candidates this year," I heard again and again. One day as I went down the hall, the door of the conference room was suddenly flung open and a teacher-friend of mine rushed out. As she passed me I glimpsed tears running down her face. Later I heard that her board had failed to pass her, and she was told she would have to try again next year.

Panic clawed my insides. This woman was a good teacher, I knew—calm, competent. What would I do under severe questioning?

The evening before my orals I was too worried to eat. For weeks I had been praying about this ordeal. That night as I dropped to my knees beside my bed I began to pray aloud. Suddenly I realized what I was saying, what I had been saying all the past weeks: "Lord, make me smart enough! Help me not to be dumb! Please, Lord, let me know the answers."

And then all at once I knew that this was not what I should be praying—not this "gimme" talk; this was not communion with God. I began to understand what I really should be talking to Him about.

"Lord, please let me reflect thy teachings as I answer those questions tomorrow. Let me show that I can be a good teacher because a knowledge of thee has helped me to know a better way of life. Help me to let my light shine. Several of these men on my board know of my religious convictions. They have known me. I have studied in their classes. I have even taught their children in high school."

Oh, I knew of the omniscience of God, but *I* was made aware of all these things as I attempted to commune with Him. And I continued, "Please, dear Lord, help me to forget myself. Help me to glorify thy name as I answer the questions."

The next morning I went very early to the education building and waited near the door of the conference room. There was an inside entrance into the room also. At the exact time appointed I went in. Five men were already seated around the large table. Another one came in from the inner door as I sat down. They all smiled and spoke to me, calling me by name.

With no preliminaries, the head of the education department turned to Mr. G. of the English department and said, "Would you like to question her first?"

My heart beat very fast. My breathing was shallow and rapid. And then a strange thing happened. I felt a warm glow in the region of my heart. My fear just seemed to flow away. I felt released and at ease.

"Mrs. Townsend, how would you teach Wordsworth?"

"I'm glad you chose Wordsworth," I said. "I often begin with his poem, 'We Are Seven.' It's in most anthologies for senior English. First I would ask the students questions something like this: What is death? What do you know about death? How would you explain death to a child? When I would begin to feel that the students were interested and begin to get responses, I would tell them, with no show of emotion, that I had to explain to my children when their father died, and I found it very difficult to know what to say. There had been seven of us—my husband and me and the five children. Then he was gone and there were no longer seven. At that point I would read the poem to the class:

. . . a simple child,
That lightly draws its breath,
And feels its life in every limb,
What should it know of death?

I met a little cottage girl:
She was eight years old, she said;
Her hair was thick with many a curl
That clustered round her head.

And on to the last lines:

'Twas throwing words away; for still
The little maid would have her will
And said, Nay, we are seven!

I would feel the students thinking with me as I read. I would not need to explain the poem after I had finished reading it.

"Then probably I would go on to 'The World Is Too Much with Us,' " I said. "To establish rapport for this one I often begin to talk about going hunting, fishing, hiking, or camping out in the open—getting away from the noise and confusion of urban life. When the students begin to respond freely, when I get them with me, I read:

The world is too much with us; late and soon,
Getting and spending, we lay waste our powers;
Little we see in Nature that is ours;
We have given our hearts away, a sordid boon. . . .

Mr. G. was leaning back in his chair, listening, and nodding his head. The other five men seemed interested.

133

"Now, Mrs. Townsend," he said, "how about teaching Burns?"

This was just as easy. I began with "A Man's a Man for A' That," but, as before, I explained how I would lay a foundation for the students to have an experience with me as I read the poem—for them to gain new insights, new concepts of life, and new understandings of people and situations.

"It's my turn," interrupted the chairman of the education department. "What would you do with a student who couldn't write essays, one who was an F student?"

"I'm sure I have made all the mistakes in the catalog, but I try very hard to find out about my students—I try to understand them—so I can teach them. For instance, a few years ago I had one fellow who couldn't grasp even the simple fundamentals of grammar. He couldn't write and couldn't spell. At first I felt that he was hopeless. But gradually, from information I gained from his essays, from little scraps of conversation that I happened to overhear, and from his responses to questions, I learned of his background. His mother had died when he was small. His father was a bartender. The boy grew up in a saloon, took his naps under the counter, helped to carry out the bottles, and learned the language of the people who frequent the bar.

"I had a glimpse of his acuity when, as we made up metaphors in class one day, he wrote, 'I shot my deer through his engine room.' True, it was crude, and he had misspelled three words in the short sentence, but I made sure that, after the spelling had been changed, this example of a figure of speech was included in our school literary magazine that month.

"When the time came for research papers to be written he stopped after school to see me. His face reflected his consternation.

" 'Missus Townsend, I can't write a paper six pages long—you know that.'

" 'Well, let's see,' I said. 'What do you really like best?'

"I was fumbling for an idea, I knew, but when he answered, 'Cars,' I grabbed onto the subject. I remembered the time I had happened into the auto mechanics shop during the class period and he had emerged from beneath an old jalopy to explain to me all about the 'innards' of his car.

" 'Of course,' I said, 'you can write something about cars.' And we were off to a start.

"Weeks later his essay came in on time. It was a treatise on the changes in the electrical connections in cars. It didn't have much literary value, but he had made wooden covers for the paper—front and back pieces—had sanded the rounded corners until they were symmetrical, had varnished the wood to a glossy surface, and had wired a spark plug to the top cover.

" 'Someone helped me proof my writing,' he admitted ruefully as he laid it on my desk."

"Don't I get a chance to question?" asked one member of the counseling department, as I paused for a moment. His question was about some intricate detail of a new test we had been giving that summer to some college students who had served as experiments for intern counseling. For a second or two I could not remember, and then again the warm feeling returned and I was able to relax and give a satisfactory answer.

The minutes went by rapidly. Several times one of my questioners said, "I know we should go on to our classes, but I want to ask another question."

More than two hours passed before they dismissed me, and I let myself out of the room and went to the library to study.

The next day as I walked to my nine o'clock class, a fellow classmate of mine—a teacher I had known for years—caught up with me and began to talk excitedly.

"Say, Elsie, what do you think Mr. F. talked about in our eight o'clock class just now? You! Oh, he didn't mention your name, but he said it was a teacher who had been taking her orals yesterday morning, and I knew the time of your appointment. He said that this person was the kind of teacher we want in our classrooms, that she reflected the ideals students should know and understand. He went on and on—most of the class period."

I did not answer—I could not. The bell rang as we slid into our seats in our classroom. I did not hear the first few minutes of the lecture. I was busy communing with my Master. I was thanking Him for letting me have this experience, for helping me to understand that education is not for ostentation, not for display. I was thanking Him for giving me this new concept of teaching, of gaining degrees, for helping me to see how my vocation could fit into His work. I was thanking Him for helping me to learn how to pray.

Family Counselor

For three school years I spent half of my time as counselor to seniors and college-bound students. What the students confided in me often shocked me so that I clutched the edge of my desk till my knuckles were white to avoid making an exclamation of dismay. I missed the hours in the classroom.

"This is not my dish," I decided and applied to teach English in the junior college in the city. "Always attempting the impossible," I chastised myself, "but it will be a learning experience."

For the first two semesters I was given the "dregs"—the night classes of remedial English, ones in which the student did not even earn college credit. But the second year the dean offered me a regular schedule.

Our students were mediocre to low in learning ability, in willingness to study and to accept responsibility for preparing lessons. Most of them worked twenty to forty hours a week on a job and tried to carry college classes. Often they were weary and sleepy when they came to class.

This college operated by the "open door" policy. Anyone could attend—"The lame, the halt, the blind," I muttered to myself sometimes. In one class I had three students in wheelchairs, paralyzed from the waist down, and two others with severe physical handicaps. I had all races and colors. We accepted everyone who applied if he had a high school diploma. Even without a diploma, a student could enter if he could pass the government education test successfully.

Day classes were somewhat more homogeneous, being composed mostly of seventeen- and eighteen-year-olds. But night classes were completely heterogeneous—from sixteen to sixty-five, their intelligence quotients as varied as their ages.

Living as I had in Montana most of my life I was completely unprepared for the animosity among people of various colors and cultures that I found in this city college. I had to adjust if I would serve. I had to learn my students so that I could relate to them. I was determined to learn to keep my "cool." Each student was interesting to me. I had always found that I must understand the person, express my interest in some way before I could teach him. But this interest took all forms.

Dennis was an example of my beginning to learn. He came into my class the first day, stopping by my desk to say, "Good afternoon, Mrs. Townsend."

Students just beginning in college rarely know a teacher's name, especially on the first day of the semester. I looked up and watched him as he found an empty desk near the front of the room. His smile exposed even, white teeth. His skin was a smooth chocolate brown, his black eyes were large and clear. A gold-colored shirt contrasted with neatly creased brown pants. Aware of my gaze he turned to me and smiled again. It was easy to return his smile.

In the weeks that followed I enjoyed his interest in the classwork. I came to rely on his accurate answers to my questions. He was eager and alert, with a quick laugh when there was humor in a discussion.

Then everything changed. Dennis Adams was absent from the Monday class. When he came into the room on

Wednesday I sensed the difference. He was defensive when I asked for assignments that were to be turned in and only mumbled some excuses.

On Friday he went to sleep before the class was over. Two fellows jabbed him in the ribs to wake him as they left the room when the period was over. He jumped, looked around dazedly, then said to me, "I'm sorry, Mrs. Townsend, but I was so tired."

The following Monday his eyes were heavy with fatigue and became almost unseeing before the class ended, although he held them wide open. He apologized for not having the assigned essay completed. For several weeks this continued. Quarter grades came out. For my class his grade was a doubtful D, not good for English composition which was a required subject.

One evening as I sat grading papers in my home, I heard the telephone ring. When I answered it I heard someone say, "Mrs. Townsend, are you a teacher at the junior college?"

"Yes," I answered.

"Do you have a boy named Dennis Adams in an English class?"

"Yes, I do."

"This is his father. Dennis' quarter grades just arrived at the house today and we are very much disturbed. Two D's and two F's!"

I began to explain. "He started out well. But the last few weeks he's been so tired, and he hasn't done his work. Have you any explanation for this?"

There was silence on the line for a moment.

"Yes. Will you try to help us, Mrs. Townsend?"

"If I can."

"Dennis has left home and is trying to support himself and keep up with a full college schedule."

"Did this happen since school began?" I asked.

"Yes, a few weeks ago. I want to tell you about it. I'm to blame for it—his leaving home, I mean. But there were many factors. And now, he won't let me talk to him, won't let me tell how sorry I am. We had a quarrel; he was insolent; I slapped him. I shouldn't have hit him, but I was angry—justly so, I thought at the time; now, I'm not so sure. He won't speak to me, just turns and walks away if I try to get near him. He hasn't been home since he walked out the door that day. He got a job, works long hours, and has a room all alone. I went to see him at his job. It's no good. Will you talk to him?"

"Mr. Adams, we have excellent counselors here who would do this better than I could. Shall I explain to them and—"

"No, I wish you'd talk to him."

"But—" I hesitated, then decided to go on, "we have one counselor who is black; perhaps he'd have better rapport."

"Mrs. Townsend, he likes you; he purposely got into your class. He had heard about you from other students before he entered the junior college. Every evening after he had been in one of your English classes, he talked to us of you, of what had happened in the class, and of your understanding of the students."

By that time I was a pushover. "Well, I'll try. What do you want me to do?"

"Persuade him to come home. Oh, and—one more thing! Don't let him know I called you."

"Okay," I answered doubtfully, "I'll see what I can do."

Over and over in my head I turned these details and tried to think how to approach the student—how to suggest a reconciliation, when I was not supposed to know of the estrangement. It seemed impossible.

The next day, after class, I laid my hand on Dennis' sleeve to detain him at the end of the class period.

"Mr. Adams, may I talk to you a moment?" I asked.

He stood quietly, looking away from me.

"Your work in this class has fallen away. Can you tell me why? Is there anything I can do? Have you been ill? You seem so weary."

"I am tired," he said. "Sleepy and tired."

"Have you been sick?"

"Not sick. But I work nine-ten hours a day on a job, cook my own meals, and do my washing and cleaning. I try to find enough time to study. Can't get all this in. I don't get much sleep."

"Must you keep a full-time job? Can't your folks help you with your college expenses?"

And then it came tumbling out—his quarrel with his father and his leaving home.

"Dad tried to treat me like an adolescent," he said, "and I'm in college. He should recognize that I'm an adult—a college student, even though I was at home. He's not fair—won't let me have any rights at all—expects me to report to him every little move I make. I can't take it. . . ."

"How long have you been on your own now?"

"Going on four weeks!"

"Do you miss your folks and your home?"

"Sure."

"Anyone in the home besides your father and mother?"

"Got a kid sister. She's cute as a button—bright, too. Say, you ought to hear the way she can imitate Sammy Davis, Jr., voice, expression, and all."

"Would you like to go back home?"

"Can't do that."

"Have you tried? Have you talked with your parents?"

"No."

"Have they tried to talk to you—to apologize?"

"I don't want to hear their mealy-mouthed nothings, just trying to get me back under their thumbs again."

"They may be very anxious about you. I'm sure your father would like to apologize, now that he's had time to think it over. Perhaps you spoke pretty sharply, too."

"I suppose I did. But he had it coming. He had no right to—"

"I won't keep you any longer, Mr. Adams, but I am concerned. I do wish you would think it over."

He nodded. Later in the week he brought in some of his makeup work, but he still looked exhausted and listless in the class period.

His father telephoned again. I told of my unsuccessful attempt.

"Is there any place you could meet your son sort of accidentally?" I asked. "Oh, say, do you attend church, Mr. Adams?"

"Yes, we do."

"Does your son go?"

"He used to go always with us. He's not been there since he left us. He's afraid of meeting us, maybe."

"I'll see if I can get him to come to church. Perhaps you could kinda bump into him there, catch him unawares."

He thanked me and ended the conversation. At school a few days later I tried to suggest the idea to Dennis Adams.

"No, I've not been going to church lately," he said.

"Why?"

"Partly because I'm tired—partly because I don't want to see the folks."

"Wouldn't you like to see your little sister and your mother? Would you go once—just try it, for me? I feel sure your family would like to see—want to know that you're okay."

Reluctantly he half-promised. Monday, after class, he stopped at my desk.

"I went," he said, "but it's no good. Saw my folks, looked at my dad. Then that big knot of resentment almost choked me. I left. Sorry, Teach!"

Each day of class he came, but halfway through the period his eyes would become cloudy with weariness, almost glassy. If I directed a question at him, the sound of his name would jerk him awake and he would ask to have the question repeated.

One evening his father telephoned again.

"Yes," he said, "we saw him at church but before we could get to the back of the room where he was sitting, he was gone."

"Have you tried to telephone him?"

"He has no telephone." He hesitated a moment. "Mrs. Townsend, has his work at college improved at all?"

"He doesn't get his assignments prepared. I'm afraid he won't make it."

The following Monday morning Dennis Adams came into class a little early, dropped several pages of written work on my desk, then took his seat. He beamed up at me, his dark eyes glowing. During the class period he was alert and eager, taking a lively part in the discussion.

"What has happened?" I wondered, wanting the class time to be over so that I could learn.

When dismissal time came I watched him put his books in his briefcase slowly and deliberately, waiting in his seat until every other student had gone. Then he came to stand beside me at the lectern.

"I'm home," he said simply.

"That's good," I said and waited.

"Dad sorta pulled a whizzer on me but I don't mind. He sent word to me that my little sister was very sick and was asking for me. I had to go. When I came in the front door, all the family stood there waiting for me. They hugged me and cried and—well—you know—"

He stopped a moment, swallowed hard. I couldn't think of anything to say.

"My sister wasn't really that sick," he went on. "But the ruse worked. Dad apologized. We had a long talk. He's promised to treat me more grown-up-like. He persuaded me to quit my job so that I could put full time on my college work. You know, Dad sure learned a lot in those weeks that I've been away from home. He's really a great guy!"

I grinned. "Could be you learned a little, too?"

He nodded and smiled and was on his way.

I'm Glad I Had a Mongoloid Child

I didn't notice her the first week of college that year. As I checked the students' names, trying to pronounce the unusual ones carefully, I was looking at the cards, listening for the part of the room from which came the answers of "Here," looking at hands raised when I did not hear answers. It was hot September; the sun beat against the brick wall of the west side of the building. This classroom was on the third floor overlooking the street. Windows were open to allow free circulation, but also let in the roar of city traffic. I accumulated little piles of damp cleansing tissue on the teacher's desk as the hour went on. My dress stuck to my back and my skin prickled with the heat. I hurried through the hour.

During the second week I handed back the essays the students had written and given to me. Each essay contained my red ink corrections. When I called the name Sally Brenton, and walked to the back of the room to give an essay into her raised hand, I noted this slender woman. She was about thirty-five or forty years of age, I judged quickly — sitting in a room filled with mostly eighteen-year-olds.

"Mrs. or Miss?" I asked, pausing.

"Mrs.," she said.

She did not look up. She was glancing over the red marks on her essay. Suddenly she raised her head, and in her eyes I read complete dismay.

To the whole class I said impersonally, "Now these errors in writing I expect, especially on the first few essays. I think you will gain much by rewriting the papers, making corrections. If I can be of any help, come to see me in my office, 100A. My conference hours are listed on that dittoed sheet I gave you the first day you came to class."

In a few days Mrs. Brenton appeared at the door of my office. Pushing aside my papers and laying my glasses on top of the stack, I motioned to a chair near my desk.

"Let's see, you're . . . ?" I began.

"Sally Brenton, from the one o'clock English 101 class," she answered.

"Oh, yes, Mrs. Brenton; how may I help you?"

"It's awful—just awful—that essay! Should I drop English? Will I make an F? I can't face my husband if I make an F. What can I do?"

"Now wait! This is your first writing for me. Tell me, how long has it been since you were in school?"

"Eighteen years! And I didn't finish high school. I got married when I was a senior."

"Then, for entry to junior college here you took the GED test?"

She nodded.

"And you must have made a good score or you'd not have been admitted."

Again she nodded.

"You want to learn—you want to go to college?"

"The doctor asked me to try it. It was his idea. I like it—I want to study. But if I'm too dumb, I'd better quit before I waste any more of my husband's money."

"He's unhappy about your coming to college?" I asked.

"Yes, damn him," she said. Her teeth were clenched and her hands were twisting in her lap.

"Why did the doctor want you to come? He must have had a good reason."

"He said that if I didn't do something to get my mind off my troubles, I'd have a complete nervous breakdown. And I mustn't do that. I have too many responsibilities. . . ." Her voice shook.

I left my desk to go to the door, closed it, and returned to my chair.

"Would you like to tell me about them?"

"I have a mongoloid child named Judy, who is three years old. I've realized she was subnormal for quite a while but tried not to think about it. She can't walk or talk or do anything for herself. My husband refuses to admit she's any different from other children. I want to take her to a special school, see what can be done for her, and learn what I can do to help her. My husband says, 'No.' I have read much literature about her and know some things that can be done.

"We have two boys in high school who are very bright. My husband has a good job. He could afford to let me take Judy to this school—this center for abnormal children. But he will not acknowledge that he has a child that is subnormal. That would be 'stooping' he thinks.

"We've quarreled over it until our home is becoming very unhappy. I've tried to soften his judgment by arguments. I've cried and begged. Finally I went to the doctor for sedatives so I could get some sleep. I was afraid I would try suicide."

She paused and waited for control. I pulled out some tissues from a box on my desk and gave them to her. She wiped her face and blew her nose.

"And he—the doctor, I mean—suggested junior college?"

"Yes and talked to my husband about it—put the fear of the devil into his arguments, I think. So here I am making a mess of it all."

"Not a mess at all. Pull your chair over here near my desk and let's look at that essay."

She took the rumpled pages from a notebook and handed them to me.

"Paper looks as if it had been bleeding! All those red marks!" she said.

Unfolding the papers on my desk, I looked quickly at the red ink writing I had done.

"I don't know what to do to rewrite it," she said. "What do you want me to do when you say, 'Use concrete imagery'? And look at this—you've written, 'These generalizations need support.' And what in the devil is a 'dangling verbal?' That's one animal I've never seen!"

She laughed nervously and I joined her heartily.

"Let's take some clean paper and rewrite the essay right here," I said.

For an hour or more we worked. She was eager and interested. At last, looking at her watch, she said quickly, "I must go now."

"Your little girl—is she at home?"

"Yes. I have a neighbor with Judy. She's promised not to tell my husband about this extra hour, but I had to talk to someone about—well, it started with English and then—"

"Ended with English," I said. "Are you taking any other classes?"

"No, just this one, and if I fail it, I'll . . ."

"You won't fail it," I said firmly. "Your mind is quick to learn. You've forgotten many things since high school days, but you'll find them coming back."

"Thank you," she said simply.

"I'll see you tomorrow in class," I said as I went to open the door for her.

A week later, as I passed back essays that had been

written in class two days before, I was aware of her quick gasp of consternation when she looked at the bright red marks on her paper. She looked down at her desk, but not before I had seen the hurt in her expressive brown eyes.

Again I invited the students to come for conferences. She came. This time she had rewritten the essay. We made additional corrections, scratching out, adding inserts, writing a different introduction, and a thesis sentence.

As she was leaving, she paused near the door.

"My husband consented to let me take Judy to the Center during the hour I am taking class, and every day at that time," she said.

"I'm glad. Let me know how she progresses," I said.

Her writing improved very slowly. She was impatient with her continued errors. Each time a paper was returned to her, she meticulously corrected the mistakes and rewrote it.

She began to adjust to the class. In reading assignments she began to respond to questions, even raising her hand to take part in the lively class discussions. Her comments were good, logically sound, and more mature than those of the eighteen-year-olds. She could see that the students did not resent her because of her age, but respected her opinions.

Often at the end of the class period I saw her leaving with another married woman about her own age.

Before the finals she came again to my office, accompanied by her friend.

"Mrs. Townsend, this semester exam, what will it be like? I'm scared of it."

"The same thing you've done a number of times before—writing an essay here in the classroom, but instead of the one hour class period you'll have the two hours listed on the exam schedule. I'll expect you to incorporate all the rules we've learned this semester."

"What about misspelled words?"

"Be sure to bring your dictionary and use it."

"Our textbook for composition?"

"Use it, too, if you like."

"But the subject?"

"I'll give many from which to choose. You'll not have difficulty, not with your varied experiences in life."

Her friend spoke up. "Did you know, Mrs. Townsend, that Sally has lost seventeen pounds this semester worrying about English class?"

"Not really!"

"Yep! She wears a size seven now."

"Don't be concerned!" Sally Brenton said. "It's a better kind of worry than I had before."

"Will you be afraid to take another class next semester?" I asked.

"Oh, no!" she answered quickly. "I think I have it licked. I've signed up for English 102 and six other credits."

"And your little girl?"

"She is learning to walk and can already say, 'Mama.' "

"Bring her in some day."

One morning in March, I heard sounds outside my office door and looked up to see Mrs. Brenton slowly leading a little girl into the room, followed by two interested students. Sitting on the chair by my desk she took her daughter on her lap and fondly pushed back the soft curly hair from the little child's face.

"This is my Judy, Mrs. Townsend," she said.

Smiling broadly I said, "Hi" to the little girl, who smiled and nodded her head.

"I'm taking her to my psych class where I will explain to the students the difficulties of teaching a mongoloid. I want them to see that I am not ashamed of Judy."

"And your husband?"

"He is beginning to understand and to accept."

During the next college year, I did not have Sally Brenton in a class. Now and then I would see her in the hall and we would chat a bit. At the end of the spring semester she came into my office and sat waiting until I had finished talking to another student.

"And now, Sally Brenton, how are you doing?"

"Great!" she said. "But I need help again. I want to go on to college—to the university. Money is my problem. Also I want to prove to my husband that I am considered of value as a student—a good risk. Can you explain to me about scholarships, loans, grants?"

"I'll do what I can and then we'll go to a counselor and he'll continue from there. In what field do you plan to major?"

"Social service, of course—psychology, handicapped children, mentally retarded, oh, something like that."

I called a counselor's office and made an appointment for her. I went to see him after Sally had gone, to brief him about her. He told me later of his success in obtaining aid for Sally.

The following semester Sally's friend came in to tell me that Sally was enrolled in the university and she was having no difficulty with her classes.

I saw her just once more, in June before her graduation. She stood by my office door and called out gaily, "Have you time for an old student, Mrs. Townsend?"

The exultant lilt of her voice, the deep glow of joy in her brown eyes, the lightness of her step and the swing of her skirts as she walked into the room, told me of her happiness.

"You bet I have," I said. I pushed the essays aside and pulled off my glasses.

"Tomorrow night I graduate from the university. I've been breaking my arm patting my back," she said.

"If you'll turn around I'll pat that straight little back of yours. Now, what are you going to do?"

"Oh, don't you know? I am going to help organize groups of parents who have mongoloid or mentally handicapped children and help them learn how to understand and teach their youngsters. It'll be great, won't it? It's been my dream, now, for two or three years."

"Wonderful! And Judy?"

"She's learned to dress herself and can say more words—and oh—many things."

She stopped and looked at me a moment and then said, "Mrs. Townsend, I'm so glad that *I* had Judy—not someone else. If I'd not had this little girl I'd not be able to do these things that I plan to do. Now, I have such a full life—and I'll have such rich, fulfilling experiences."

Erika

A letter from my daughter, Marilyn, who was a student in the University of Tubingen in Germany began a series of events that added much to my knowledge of students. The letter read, "Since all four of your daughters are now away from home, you need a girl around. [Like I do a hole in the head! I thought.] I have invited Erika, a student friend here, to come live at our home and attend the university there in the city. She wants to go to college in America for a year."

I sputtered and gasped, but continued to read.

"She's sent a transcript of her credits to the university. Will you use your influence to get them evaluated right away so she can get her application for a visa accepted? Okay? We'll be arriving in August. I'll let you know the exact dates later. We booked our passage to New York City on the big German liner 'Berlin.' I think then we'll stop to visit in Ohio on our way home."

Filled with consternation, I began to list mentally the reasons—or excuses—for refusing to accept this German girl in our home for a year.

"If I didn't have a wishbone instead of a backbone . . ." I mumbled inanely to my husband, knowing I would call the registrar at the university the next day.

At the railroad depot in August I waited, eager to see my daughter, skeptical about the new guest who would be arriving with her. Marilyn came through the doors first, her shoulders sagging with the weight of her suitcases. Behind her was a tall girl with short blond hair, a pair of snow skis over her shoulders, ski boots dangling across her chest.

"Mother, this is Erika Mecklenbeck," my daughter introduced as she set down the heavy luggage and put her hand on my shoulder.

"*Guten Tag,*" I enunciated clearly.

"Oh, Mom, she speaks English fluently."

"I am glad to meet you," Erika said with a British accent, extending her hand and catching mine in a firm, muscular handshake.

"Your trunks?" I asked.

Marilyn held out baggage checks.

The first two weeks were easy with my daughter at home to chat with Erika in English or in German, but Marilyn left for a distant university to complete her graduate work. After that I was on my own. My husband and I took Erika to the state fair. We walked through the exhibits of animals, rode the ferris wheel, and ate hot dogs and cotton candy. She was eager, filled with curiosity, and completely uninhibited.

Then college classes began. Erika rode to the university every day with another student who lived near us. If her classes or her study in the library prevented her returning with him, she took a city bus to my college and sat waiting in my office until I returned there from my classes, then rode home with me. Easily she fitted into university life.

But at our home it was different. She had never cooked a meal or washed a dish. She knew nothing about sewing, washing, or ironing. In her home in Germany a maid had attended to all that. The "woolies" of dust accumulated under her bed until I explained about housecleaning. She was willing—just inexperienced.

154

"What shall I call you?" she asked.

"Why not call me Elsie and my husband Wendell?" I suggested.

Wendell adjusted to her ways easily. He joked with her, teased her, and treated her more like a sister. With my mother, who was elderly and becoming senile, she was at ease at once. Erika petted her, and called her *Grossmutter* or Grandma, and laughed at her eccentricities.

At the university she delighted the professors, especially in the literature courses. Fluent in speaking five languages and able to read eight, she was familiar with the writings of the great authors of the world. She had studied most of their works in the original languages. Often, however, she came to me to ask about rephrasing her thoughts, reaching for the exact diction for the idioms of our language.

She enjoyed the fellowship of the students at the university. "Erika has never met a stranger," I told my husband. She was cosmopolitan, having studied one summer at a university in England, another at the Sorbonne in France, and having traveled over most of continental Europe.

But when she spoke derisively about the immaturity of the average student in American colleges, her arrogance made me instantly defensive. Often I thought I detected a ring of the philosophy of the "super race."

Erika loved the sun and the warmth of the fall days. On Saturdays she would pull on shorts and a blouse and spread a blanket on the grass of the lawn. Lying flat on her stomach she studied her lessons, then dozed awhile. The third day of this she came to me scratching and rubbing several red welts on her legs and abdomen.

"You must have slid off the blanket a little," I said. "I warned you of chiggers."

"Chiggers? What kind of animals are they?"

"Very tiny insects—so small you seldom see them. You must not lie on the grass until after a frost has killed them."

"Those little animals! They spoil my fun!" But she kept off the grass after that.

Classes at the university were always dismissed before the middle of December for a three-week holiday season.

"Erika," my husband suggested at breakfast in early December, "would you like to go to my brother's place in Montana and go skiing for a week in the mountains there?"

"That I'd like," she said, her blue eyes lighting up.

"We'll write to him, but I am sure it'll be okay. You can go by train. There are two good ski resorts near Bozeman."

Two weeks later, she boarded the train, carrying her heavy skis. As she deftly maneuvered the awkward slats through the door of the coach, she turned to wave and smile.

"Auf wiedersehen!" she called.

"Auf wiedersehen!" we answered. "Have fun!"

A week later we met her at the depot. Her skin was burned a reddish-brown, her smile full of the joy of living.

"That first day," she said after we had stowed her gear in the car and started home, "I got up to the top of the ski lift up Bridger Canyon and then I was in a panic."

"So I heard," Wendell said and chuckled. "My brother called us."

"But, Erika, you've been in the Alps. Our mountains shouldn't have scared you."

"I kept telling myself that," she said, "but I was afraid of that steep drop down the long, high mountain."

"Did you make it down by yourself?"

"People helped me. They were kind. But after that first time, everything was okay."

"Did you go every day?"

"All but one. That day, Wendell, I went to the ranch to

see your mother and father. That was good—*sehr gut!* I like them!"

All my family had arrived for the holidays by then. Marilyn and Erika rattled off their conversation in Deutsch. Erika admitted to having had some *Heimweh*—"Homesickness, Daddy," Marilyn explained to Wendell.

On Christmas Eve we gathered in the living room for our traditional family reading. On the back of the grand piano two large candles softly lighted the handcarved figures of the nativity scene which Marilyn had bought for me in Tubingen. A fat red candle on each side of the music rack gave a flickering light. On the arm of the davenport another candle added to the dim illumination of the room.

"Erika," I said, handing her the open Bible, "you read the Christmas story here in Luke where I have marked it."

I gave her the big candle from the davenport. Her voice rang out in the complete quiet of the room, "And it came to pass that . . ." and on to the end of the passage.

"Jim, it's your turn to offer the prayer for us all," I ordered in my best matriarchal manner.

When he had finished, Marilyn began to play the first notes of a familiar tune and we sang the Christmas carols, then drifted on to "White Christmas," "Silver Bells," and many other songs of the holiday.

In January the between-semester break offered another vacation for Erika.

"You want to see America, Erika. Why not go to my brother's in Needles, California, this time?" I suggested. "It's warm enough for you there!"

"Ach so! I know the one—the *Herr Doktor, nicht wahr?* Yah, I go."

We helped her plan details and again took her to the railroad depot. In a week she returned, her blonde hair

157

bleached almost white from the sun, her skin smoothly brown, and her eyes spilling over with joy.

"*Schon!*" she said enthusiastically, as soon as she could get through the swinging doors and into the railroad lobby. "I had fun!"

"What did you do? Where did you go?" we asked as we walked toward the car.

"One day we went to Death Valley, pulling the trailer house behind us. We slept all night there. The stars are so bright. It is so quiet—no sound at all."

"And hot!"

"That I like!"

"Did you get to see the Pacific Ocean?"

"Yes, and swim in it, too. We went to San Francisco, rode the trolley car, ate at Fisherman's Wharf, and drove past Cannery Row. What many things I can tell when I go to my home!"

One Saturday morning Erika came into the kitchen, rubbing her eyes sleepily.

"*Fur Fruhstuck* yet?" I joked. "This is a bit early for you, isn't it?"

She dropped into her accustomed chair at the table and poured herself a cup of coffee.

"What brought you out at this time on a Saturday morning?" Wendell asked.

"I must be at the university by ten thirty. Our concert choir—you know I sing with them—is performing at the big hotel downtown for that government meeting. You read about it in the papers. All the big men from your capital will be there and many ambassadors from other countries." She turned to me. "You will take me there this morning?"

"This is a bad day for me," I answered. "I must take Mother to the doctor's office at nine for an appointment.

And I may have to take her to the hospital and leave her there for a day or two. But I can sandwich this in somehow. Can you manage to get back from the city by yourself? Remember, even from down in the city the buses don't come over to our area after a certain hour on Saturday. Call me if you don't get a ride home."

"I'll be okay if you get me to the auditorium of the art gallery. We sing a concert there at first. Then we go to the big hotel in the downtown city. But I can ride with one of the students to the hotel."

Hastily I dressed, drove to my mother's house, helped her tie her shoes and comb her hair, and drove her to the medical building. The doctor was still busy with another client. I went to the desk.

"I must leave my mother here for a while," I whispered to the woman in charge there. "Keep an eye on her until I get back, will you? She sometimes forgets and wanders off."

She smiled and nodded. Running down the stairs, I hurried to my car, drove home, and then took Erika to the art gallery near the university campus. Back at the medical building again, I found that Mother had to be taken to the hospital for a checkup. Getting her admitted, filling pages of entrance forms, and helping her get settled in her rooms took a long time.

I warned the nurses of her "wandering" habits. She loved the nurses, enjoyed going to the hospital. They petted her, but also scolded her gently.

"Mother, take your hat off," I said as I stood at the door.
"Why?"

"You're going to stay awhile."

"Oh, yes," she said. She handed her hat to a nurse who then began to talk to her, motioning for me to leave. I slipped out the door.

It was late that night before Erika returned. Twice I got up to look at the clock, concerned about her being in the city alone. At one o'clock I heard the front door open and footsteps in the hall.

"Erika," I said softly.

"*Ach,* so! I waken you? Then I can tell you."

I came out into the hall.

"I can turn on the light here so I can show you what I have?"

She held out to me a table napkin on which were written many names. Even in the dim light of the hall I could see her starry eyes. Her excitement spilled over into her voice.

"What's this, Erika?"

"At the convention when we sing, I saw the ambassador from my home, from Deutschland. I went to him and told him who I am. He was glad to talk with me and introduced me to others there—from Japan, Italy, Washington, D.C., and many places. Since I speak their languages, they asked me to the banquet table as a guest for the evening to translate for them. I went and sat beside a former president of the United States. I talked with many famous people. See, here, they autographed my napkin for me."

With awe I read one well-known name after another.

"Weren't you afraid?" I asked her.

"What's to be afraid of? They were very nice to me."

"Oh, Erika, Erika, you're priceless," I said. "Now hurry off to bed."

"I go," she said happily.

When college classes were nearing their close in June, Erika began to talk of her return to Germany. My brother who lives near us heard her.

"Erika," he said, "how would you like to go with our family to Alaska?"

160

"I would like that!" she responded instantly.

"I'll make a bargain with you. If you'll work in my Fourth of July fireworks stand for the two weeks and supervise the kids a bit, I'll take you with us."

"When do we go?"

"We leave early in the morning on the fifth of July."

"And when do you come back?"

"In about six weeks, we plan. We have a new car-bus that sleeps eight. We will drive to Seattle, then north on the highway to Alaska."

"I go," she said firmly, *"danka."*

We received postcards from her as she journeyed west and north. In August she returned, babbling of catching salmon, the airplane trip to the Arctic circle, the tremendous mountains they flew over, and the drive back on the Alcan Highway. They had kissed the surface of the blacktop when they finally came to the end of the rough-graveled roads.

I had already shipped her luggage to New York. That night we put her on a plane and said good-bye.

"Auf wiedersehen," she said. "You will come to see me sometime?"

"We will try," we said. *"Auf wiedersehen!"*

Ankar Nagasa

My attention was drawn to this handsome student from the very first day he entered one of my classes. His skin was brown, smooth, and unblemished. His flashing smile lighted up his large black eyes. His name was so unusual that I spelled it out as I read the class roll and asked him to pronounce it. Ankar Nagasa!

"From what country?" I asked.

"I came from Iran," he answered in careful English, but his accent was noticeable.

He sat in one of the chairs over by the window. The second class day he was absent. The next day he was there. I heard him talking to a neighboring student about the assignment.

"Did you do anything in class Wednesday?" he asked. "I didn't miss anything important, did I?"

"We wrote an essay."

He seemed undisturbed that he had missed the day's work. Several days later he brought an essay to class and gave it to me.

"But the writing you missed was done in class period," I said. "You must make up that essay by coming to my office and doing it."

He did not answer, only shrugged when I handed back the paper he had just given me. But he did not come to my office to make it up. His attendance continued erratic—absent one or two classes, present now and then. On the first class test he made a very low F.

Two weeks later, during a test, I caught him cheating, reprimanded him, and took away his paper. The next out-of-class essay assignment he brought no writing at all. When I asked him about the omission, he shrugged, smiled engagingly and gave a vague excuse.

For weeks this continued. In my grade book I had a row of F's after his name. I went to see a counselor.

"Mr. Nagasa is here on a student visa," he explained. "Last spring he married one of our girls, a beautiful young woman—an honor student. But this fellow is a scamp. He's trying to get citizenship papers through his marriage to her."

"How about his grades in other classes?"

"No good! That's why he's taking English 101 again. He flunked it before."

"What does he do for finances?"

"His wife has a job and still keeps her grades high enough so that she is on the dean's list. As far as I know he's earned no money. You can see him in the poolroom of the student union most of the day."

"And the girl?"

"She has too much pride to admit defeat."

Toward the end of the semester I assigned a research paper to be written by each student, fifteen hundred to two thousand words, carefully footnoted in formal style. On a designated day each student was to bring his choice of subject; next time, a list of available resources; next note cards filled out, an outline, then a rough draft, and finally the finished paper. Each item I checked carefully, often having individual conferences with the students. For each of these assignments Ankar brought nothing.

163

On the day the finished papers were turned in, my desk was piled high with folders by the students. My arms were filled with the papers as I went to my office.

The following day, having two hours free in succession, I picked up a stack of folders and went to the conference room on the second floor. It was quiet and no one would think to look for me there. Two long tables had been placed end to end, with chairs spaced along each side of the entire length. I dropped into a chair at the far end of the table and carefully laid down my armful of folders. Across the table from me was another teacher, assiduously checking math papers. She looked up, smiled, and returned to her task. Farther down the long table two girls studied quietly, not even looking up at my entrance.

At random I chose a research essay, read it slowly, marked it, and reached for another one. On the title sheet I read, "The Need for More Parks in America," by Ankar Nagasa. I began to read. Suddenly I remembered that he had turned in no rough draft, no note cards. I checked my grade book to make sure. I went back to the essay. It was astounding—a very well-written paper, carefully footnoted, with excellent diction and a well-developed thesis idea. About halfway through the paper I stopped.

Mumbling to myself, I wrote at the top of the first page of the essay, "See me about this essay. Did you write it yourself? Where are your note cards? Your rough draft?"

Hearing my muttering, the math teacher lifted her head.

"This makes me furious!" I said aloud. "I'm sure this student did not write this essay. He's done no acceptable work at all this whole semester. He couldn't have changed so suddenly. But how can I prove it?"

"Do you think he copied it from someone?"

"I don't know. Each semester we English teachers burn

the students' rough drafts and note cards, and return only their finished papers. But he failed to bring his rough draft at all—or his note cards. Of course there's the possibility that he copied it from a short article in the *Reader's Digest* or another periodical."

The other teacher made sympathetic sounds.

"Since he's a foreign student we try to give extra consideration, but this has gone too far."

I slapped down the essay, picked up another research paper, and began to read. I was aware that the two girls quietly stacked their books and went out of the room. For about a half hour or more there was no sound but the rustling of pages and the scratching of ball-point pens.

Suddenly I heard a disturbance at the door. One of the girls who had been in the room before was literally pushing Ankar Nagasa through the doorway. Her face was flushed and her eyes burned with anger and shame.

"You tell her," she said.

His eyes looking toward the floor, he said nothing.

"If you don't, I will," she menaced.

Still he made no sound.

"Mrs. Townsend, this is my husband." She cut the words off, bringing her teeth down upon each syllable. "I made him admit just now what he did. He got up into the top shelf of the clothes closet of our apartment and stole my essay. He copied it word for word and handed it to you for his own writing. I didn't know until I guessed when I heard you talking about the paper you were grading. I'm so sorry—oh, you don't know how sorry I am!"

She dropped her hand from his shoulder, turned and ran from the room, the sound of her sobs following her down the hall.

I tried to question Ankar. He said not a syllable, just

stood with downcast eyes. At last he went away. Later that day I went again to the counselor, telling him of the episode.

"What would you advise me to do?" I asked.

"We've had notices from all his instructors that he's doing failing work. He won't be accepted here for college work again. And his record will prevent his entering any other college."

"But his wife?"

"I don't know—just got taken in, I suppose, by his charm. It is one of those unfortunate marriages. He is attractive and debonair. Perhaps she thought it was a challenge, a dare. So many girls marry a young scoundrel hoping to reform him. It doesn't work. I'll see that she gets a scholarship or a loan if I can, but as for him . . ." He shrugged his shoulders. "Don't be disturbed, Mrs. Townsend."

Ankar did not return to class. I threw his paper into the wastebasket.

Girl from Unwed Mothers' Home

At Junior College we had to teach night classes almost every semester—in addition to our day classes. One semester I found I had been scheduled to use a classroom that had originally been used for science demonstration purposes. On a platform a long marble tabletop took the place of the ordinary teacher's desk. Indented in this was a large sink with two faucets at one end. A gas burner facility, racks for test tubes, and various other iron apparatus were part of necessary science equipment on the table.

The desks were filled with a large class of students, leaving the platform the only place for me to stand, with the big demonstration table between me and my class. My short stature—five feet and two inches, if I stretch—did not make this arrangement any more convenient.

As usual in a night class, the students were varied. But before many class periods had passed I had soon learned to know them from their essays—their interests, their backgrounds, their goals, and their hangups. Except for one student this group seemed not too unusual. There were several who worked for a big manufacturing company that would pay their tuition if they attended, a few who had flunked out and were now on probation, and two policemen who came in uniform with their big guns bulging at their sides. A few mothers of small children attended while the fathers took care of the children at night.

But one girl was different. Anne Carson was about twenty years old, I judged; nothing unusual about that. It was her appearance. Her straw-textured hair was black at the roots, blonde at the ends, and brittle from inexpert bleaching. Her blouse and skirt were cheap, faded, and mismatched. Blotches and pits on the skin of her face suggested former acne or improper diet. She was awkward and ill at ease.

But I soon discovered that she knew English rhetoric. The beginning of the semester was a review. Often she was the only one in the room who understood dangling modifiers, ambiguous reference, or incorrect syntax.

Her first essay shocked me completely and sent me rushing to the counselor's office the next day to look at her records. Dramatically vivid, her writing had told of personal knowledge of homosexuality and of a friend who had been deliberately promiscuous. She had described in detail the night's experience and the ensuing abortion.

On her records I found a mother's name, but only an empty space in the line given for the father's name. Her address was the "home for wayward girls." I could get no more information from the counselor except that she had been allowed to come to the college for night courses. She did secretarial work in the "home."

In class she soon began to be bored by the tempo. Progress was slow because of the remedial work required for the other students.

"Is this all we're going to do—this silly sixth-grade stuff?" she asked me one evening after class.

"Why not turn in a few extra essays?" I suggested.

"I can choose my own subject matter?"

I nodded.

She did. There were stories of smoke-filled bars, of two men drinking, fondling each other, and leaving for a back room. She described the skillful methods of stealing from stores, and told of girls in trouble. The imagery was so vivid that I experienced each detail, feeling as if I should wash my eyes after reading them. I felt sure that she was writing from experience, not from imagination. Just to read her stories was a traumatic experience for me. But she had the rare gift of turning a phrase, and making it original in its expression.

After class one evening I stopped her as she started out the door.

"Miss Carson, may I talk to you a minute?"

An expression of panic filled her eyes. I could almost feel her wince as if I had struck her.

"What did I do now?" she said sharply.

"You have written very well—that's what you did," I said and smiled.

She said nothing, did not move at all.

"Would you like to take some tests?" I asked.

"Tests!" she repeated. "What kind of tests? Why do I have to take them? I don't trust tests."

"These tests are to prove to you how very intelligent you are! I don't think you are aware that you are a very unusual person with special talents."

"Whoof!" she scoffed.

"Also there are tests that will help you to examine your interests, your personality, and your strengths."

She shook her head. "I don't want things written down on my record."

"No recording will be done, I promise you, unless you want it."

"Where do I have to go to take the tests?"

"I'll make an appointment with a counselor. . . ."

She drew away from me and interrupted me.

"Why do I have to see a counselor?"

"He'll show you how to take the tests and tell you the purpose of each one. Then, after you have finished, he'll score them, show you the scores, explain them, and help you to take a look at yourself."

"I'm not sure I want to take a look at myself."

"You'll learn many good things, I know," I said, trying to convince her.

"But I can't be here early to take them."

"How about during this class period? You're just spinning your wheels on what we're doing now. I could make an appointment for you."

"Okay. You talked me into it."

I spoke to Mr. Herman, the counselor who would be in his office on those particular nights. For three class periods of an hour and a half each she reported to him instead of to my room. A day or two after the tests were completed, Mr. Herman called me.

"You have a free period, Mrs. Townsend?" he asked.

"When?"

"Right now. I looked up your schedule. If you aren't too busy with something else, I want to talk to you about your night student that I've been testing."

"Be right down!"

Not waiting for the elevator, I ran down the flights of stairs and went breathless into his office. The counselor placed several folders before me, his face beaming.

"Take a look at these scores on ability tests—ninety-nine percentile in each field except math, and ninety percentile in that! Are you satisfied?"

"Boy!" I yelped. "That's great! And I was right. Now the other scores."

For an hour we interpreted and discussed. I told him of the essays, of her environment, the evident experiences of her life, and the lurid life about which she wrote so vividly.

In the next evening class I watched for Anne Carson. She was so quiet; it seemed to me that some of the pugnacious expression was gone from her face. Once she looked at me directly and I thought I felt a communication pass between us. She dropped her gaze as if embarrassed.

After class I stopped her and began to bubble over with my enthusiasm about her tests.

"Now aren't you glad you tried those tests?"

"What does it prove?" she said, shrugged me off, and left the room.

Several times I attempted to build her ego, but failed completely. The second semester she was in my English Comp II class and also in a world literature course taught by another teacher. After a few weeks I began to suggest to the girl that she plan to carry a full load of college credits by coming to day classes.

"I can't," she said. "I'm no longer required to stay at the 'home' but I have no place to go so I've been working full time in the office as secretary. This gives me my board and room and a little money for paper and pencils each week."

"Your mother lives here in the city?"

"Yes, but she wouldn't have me. I'd spoil her trade. Having a daughter my age around would cramp her style."

"Well . . ." I was temporarily out of arguments.

Another evening I tried again, offered to ask the counselor to try to get a government loan, perhaps a scholarship.

Defensively she said finally, "Mrs. Townsend, you've got me all wrong. I'm not really smart. Besides I'd never get accepted into regular college schedule. If you'd see my high school record you'd know they wouldn't take me."

"But I did see it."

"You did? Did you see that F I got in freshman algebra—got mad at the teacher and goofed off all semester!"

"So what!"

"That would make a college not want to let me in!"

"Don't be silly! The A you got in last semester college English and the two A's you are getting now will prove that you're capable of doing college work and willing to do it."

"You're kidding!"

"Go ask the counselor."

She did and began to accept his help. The evening of the final semester exam I waited at the door to talk with the girl.

"You won!" she said.

"I did? How?"

"I've been accepted in the university. Mr. Herman found out about my grandma—helped persuade her to let me live with her while I go to college. That'll take care of board and room. The government loan will pay for tuition and books. I can earn the rest."

I was grinning like a Cheshire cat. She started out the door, then turned to say, "And I suppose you'll want ten percent of the royalties when my books begin to sell." She laughed joyously.

I Learn Tolerance

Usually I don't teach in the summer, so when a call came in August I was home to receive it.

"This is Mr. Larsen of the People to People Program," he said. "Could you take guests from Denmark for a week in your home?"

"When?" I asked.

"August 17-23."

"How many?"

"At least two. Four if you can."

"I can take two, but if I take more they would have to sleep in the recreation room in the basement."

"That's okay. We have two students—boys—and also a veterinarian and his wife. We'll send you their names and pictures right away. You're to meet them at the Memorial Building at nine o'clock the morning of August 17. There will be one hundred and two Danish people in this group, coming on buses. They've had a week's stay in Illinois."

"Do they speak our language?"

"Very well."

"What are we supposed to do?"

"We have certain activities planned for them as a group. But most of the time they will just be in your home. Be yourselves—be natural. We'll send you a copy of the week's activities."

"Okay," I said weakly and hung up the receiver. I began to plan.

In a few days the pictures of the four Danish members of People to People arrived. I tried to pronounce their names. Jens Søndergaard! Bjørn Petersen! Helge and Margarethe Grønholt-Pedersen. I read in the encyclopedia for hours about the culture of the people of Denmark, their history, mythology, and customs.

The morning of the seventeenth of August was hot and humid. I thought of the cool climate of Denmark and checked the air conditioner of our house before I left for the Memorial Building. In the car on the front seat beside me I had placed a large placard which was fastened to a long wooden slat. On it I had printed "I am Elsie Townsend."

The big Greyhound buses were just pulling to the curb as I drove up. Getting out of the car, I stood under a tree near the sidewalk holding my sign high. The travelers milled out of the buses, then began to walk down the sidewalks on both sides of the street.

A couple approached me, read my name on the placard, and then hurried over to me.

"We are Helge and Grethe Grønholt-Pedersen."

"I am Elsie Townsend. I am so glad to meet you. You are to go with me to my house you know."

"Yes, that is true." It was the man who answered. He put his tiny cigar in his mouth and puffed vigorously on the cheroot.

"I am also looking for two college fellows," I said. "One is named Jens Søndergaard. He is a medical student in Copenhagen. The other is Bjørn Petersen, who lives in Slagalse."

"Oh, we live near Slay-el-see," the woman said.

"Is that how the word is pronounced?" And I laughed at

myself. I showed her Bjørn's picture with Slagalse printed below his name. She nodded.

Just then a tall fellow with sandy hair, pink complexion, and brown freckles waved in my direction and pointed to my sign. I nodded and waved.

"Bjørn Petersen," he called, pointing to himself.

"Elsie Townsend," I yelled, pointing to myself.

As we were shaking hands another Danish traveler moved near us. He was very blond, with the bluest eyes. He set down his brown suitcase.

"I think I have found the right one," he said. "I am Jens Søndergaard. You are my family here?"

"Yes, we're all together now. Here's my car. We'll put the luggage in the trunk."

In a few minutes we were in the car and I began to weave the vehicle in and out of the traffic.

"We'll be comfortable in here in a short time," I apologized. "It takes a few minutes for the car air conditioner to cool us completely."

I asked them where they had stopped on their way from New York and how many days they had been in the United States. Their English was very good. I marveled at their mastery of our language.

"From the fourth grade on we study it," they said.

"Now, let's see. Have you been told of your itinerary here for this week?"

"A little," Helge said.

"I understand we will all meet for a luncheon given you by the Rotary Club on Wednesday; go to an old Indian fort by the river on Tuesday; and Friday evening we will have a good-bye picnic in the city park. This much I know. Are there any special things you'd like to see or do while you are here?"

"One day I go shopping in the stores," Grethe answered.

"Any girls that aren't afraid of strange students?" Bjørn said and grinned ingenuously. "I'd like to date an American girl."

"I know some student nurses that I can trust," I said. "I'll call them and match you two up for an evening. Oh, about laundry. Do you have clothes you'd like to wash?"

All four began to speak at once—then laughed.

"I'll manage the washing for all four," Grethe offered.

Soon we were coming up the driveway to our house.

"What wonderful trees," Helge said. "So big; so tall. How old are some of them?"

"One of them is over a hundred years old, I think. We bought the land years ago and built our house here because of the beautiful trees. *Schone, nicht waht?*" I said proudly.

"*Sprechen Sie Deutsch?*" he said quickly.

"*Nur wenige Worten,*" I said. "I studied German in college, but I have forgotten the vocabulary."

I showed them their rooms and then we walked out onto our patio. I led them to the garden so they could see the fruit trees and the grape vineyard.

The next day my husband and I took them to church with us; after dinner we drove for hours, pointing out places of interest. On Monday when the others went shopping Jens did not go. He did not even come to breakfast. Later he came into the kitchen where I was planning the evening meal.

"Jens, you've had nothing to eat. Let me get you something."

"*Na, tag scitta hah!*—that's no thank you in Danish," he said. "But I am not hungry. I feel sick."

He touched his abdomen. Until almost noon, he lay on the davenport in the living room, then came into the kitchen where I was making sandwiches for our lunch.

"Could you help me call Denmark?" he asked hesitatingly. "I could tell them to let the cost be paid there."

"Yes, of course. What time is it at your home now?"

"Six o'clock in the evening. My girl will be back from her work. I want to talk to her."

On a piece of paper he wrote the name and number and began to teach me to pronounce it correctly.

"That mark on the letter O is almost like the German umlaut, but not quite. Try to say it," he said.

I practiced awhile, then called the overseas operator and explained. In a few minutes someone spoke in Danish. Quickly I gave Jens the receiver.

He talked rapidly, his face transforming as he spoke. When the three minute warning was given, he said good-bye. He turned to me, his eyes shining, and said with lilting voice, "My girl! I have the *heimweh* for her—how you say it? home longing for her. Now I am okay."

"And are you ready to eat lunch with me? You are hungry now?"

"Yes, I will eat gladly."

It was a busy week. When we took our new friends to the buses and told them good-bye, they said, "Not good-bye—*auf wieder sehen*," and smiled.

"That's good—*auf wieder sehen*," I agreed.

"What's it mean?" my husband asked.

"Until we meet again."

"You will come to Denmark to see us sometime, *vielleicht?*" they asked.

"We would like to do that," I assured them.

"And come to København to visit me too?" Jens asked.

"If we should come we will want to see much of Denmark. But we have never traveled much. Maybe someday. . . ."

After our guests had gone, we stood talking together.

"Why don't we accept their invitation?" someone asked.

"What?"

"Go to Denmark and visit in their homes—let them return the hospitality. The People to People organization there has offered to reciprocate with us. And the air lines and buses will give us a special rate."

The idea caught fire. Four times we met that winter, to plan a trip to Europe for the following summer. By May we had twenty-nine people signed up to make the tour. One member was a former citizen of Denmark who had come to America to attend college years ago, had married and still lived here. He offered to be our guide. He still spoke the language of the Danes fluently.

For a little extra expense we found that we could take some side trips, besides the stay in Denmark. We made out our itinerary and remade it. We learned to sing the Danish national anthem in the native language, learned to say thank-you and please—all the simple amenities.

In June we boarded the big plane and flew across the Atlantic Ocean. Our first stop was Oslo, Norway. Two days there, then to Belgium, and then we went by bus through Germany, Austria, and to Zurich, Switzerland. Wendell and I rented a small car and started off on our own, promising to meet the group at Copenhagen a week later.

Carefully following a map of Germany we drove north to Tubingen where we stayed with Erika, my German girl, and her husband. They went with us to a great castle high on a hill. The Hohenzollern family still lived in part of the castle. We explored the well-preserved feudal halls, the towers, the dungeons, the armor room and gazed fascinatedly at the crown jewels. We crossed the moat on the drawbridge, and looked up at the huge portcullis.

The next morning we were on our way again, this night to stop at Solingen with Erika's parents. Another day and we had reached Kiel, where we checked in the car and bought tickets to ride on the railroad to Copenhagen. Getting on the train was easy. I knew a few German words. But at the Danish border we had to change trains. A German trainman directed us to the car to board. Sitting in the little compartment, we watched the landscape flow by, then became aware of the woman and two children opposite us, eating lunch from a basket.

"Hey, look," Wendell called to me. "We're coming to the ocean. Now what?"

Up an incline the train went, onto a bridge, traveling over the water for miles, then onto another Danish island and across that island. When we reached the ocean again, the train stopped. Someone motioned for us to get off.

"Here's where we get on a big boat," I said, "but which one? Where is the ship that goes to Zeeland?" I said to the porter.

"Nah," he said and shook his head.

"Wo ist der shippe nach Copenhagen?" I said in fragmented German.

Someone tapped me on the shoulder. I turned around. Behind me stood a tall grey-haired woman who asked, *"Sprecken zie Deutsch?"*

"Wenige," I stuttered.

"Gehen sie mit mir," she said and led the way. Following her closely we went down the steps of the train, along the wharf, and up the gangplank onto a small ocean liner. Our heavy suitcases bumped against our legs as we walked along. We entered a large room. At the end of the room I saw a big placard and an arrow. In bold letters was printed Essen Raum.

"Haben sie Mittag Essen?" I asked, knowing my syntax was dreadful.

"Nein," she said.

"Essen sie mit uns?" I begged.

"Ich mochte gern," she said, and led us to the expansive dining room where many people were seated at tables. There was a ceiling to the room, but the sides were open and we looked out on the ocean.

She translated the menu into German and helped us order our meal. As we waited we tried to converse. We learned that she was Swedish, German and Danish being additional languages for her. She was returning to her home in Marme, Sweden, across the bay from Copenhagen.

The rays from the bright sun glistened on the quiet blue water as our ship moved away from the port and out to sea. For a half hour or more there was no sight of land. Then we caught glimpses of the roofs of houses on the island of Zeeland. We had finished our meal and were walking the decks when we came near the land.

When the ship docked we found our suitcases and stood in line to disembark. As we waited we began to ask information about what to do to get on another train.

"We have a ticket to Copenhagen," I explained, using my crude German. "But on the way to Copenhagen, we want to stop and visit people at Slagalse."

She pointed to a sign at the railroad terminal. "Take that Copenhagen train, see?"

I nodded. She had gone ahead. Suddenly she turned, ran back to us.

"No," she said in German, "not that train. It does not stop at all. Here," and she led us down the steps to the train below the ground. She paused long enough to be sure we were on the right train, then ran back up the steps.

We called, *"Danke schon,"* and waved.

Boarding our train, we took out notebooks and began to plan what to do when we arrived in Slagalse.

"Here's the telephone number of the Grønholt-Pedersens," I said. "We'll call them from the depot when we get there."

"Didn't you tell them just when we'd get there?" my husband asked.

"I couldn't—didn't know the train schedule. But they promised to come as soon as we telephoned them."

Leaving the train at Slagalse, we went into the station, found telephones, and Wendell began to dial. I leafed through the telephone book.

"Bjørn Petersen lives right here in town," I said. "I'll find his phone number and we can talk to him while we wait for the Pedersens to get here."

I turned the pages of the telephone book. "Petersen . . . Petersen," I mumbled. "Wendell, there are hundreds and hundreds of Petersens. I can't tell which one . . . why, there's an alphabetization of the first names, then another set of pages of Petersens with the same first names. I don't understand."

He laughted at my consternation. We went outside to wait for our Danish friends. A car drove up and stopped beside the curb. We recognized Grethe and Helge and called out greetings. They took us to their home.

For three days they drove us over the flat surface of the Danish countryside. By the ocean we saw the fishermen bringing in big black eels. In a building nearby Helge bought a smoked eel and took it home for our supper. Recoiling inwardly I ate the sliced meat. One day they took us to a little whitewashed stone church that is over nine hundred years old. In the nave, painted on the ceiling and the walls, is the scene of the crucifixion. Instead of Roman soldiers, there were Vikings who nailed Jesus to the cross.

Another day Bjørn joined us in Slagalse and we went to the Moulin Rouge Restaurant for smorgasbord. We shopped in the stores in the town. Wendell bought a shiny carafe—a thermos. I bought picture plates—of the ship we rode on, of the big windmills, of the thatched-roofed cottages, and of Rothskilde Cathedral.

Sunday morning we drove the sixty miles to this cathedral and attended the early services. Afterwards Grethe and Helge guided us all over the edifice. We paused in wonder before the sarcophagi of Danish kings and queens, marveled at a great gold altar.

"We were both christened here and had our first communion. Helge was a choir boy. And of course our wedding vows were taken in this chapel," Grethe explained.

"Stand still, now," Helge said as we came back to the entrance. "Look up over the door at the antique clock. The knight is Saint George. The beast is a dragon. Watch what happens as the clock nears the hour."

With fascination we looked at the figures. Suddenly the dragon moved, the knight struck, the beast made a sound like a squeak. The clock began to strike.

"For hundreds of years," Helge explained, "it was operated by weights. Now all is done by electricity."

Early in the morning we left Slagalse. Riding along in the train we stood at the windows and gazed and pointed.

"Over there," Wendell said. "A sign—Odense—isn't that the town where Hans Christian Andersen was born?"

I whipped off the cover of the camera and began to focus.

"If we slow down," I said, "I'll snap a picture."

I did, but got only the big sign, Odense.

In Copenhagen I held out to a taxi driver the printed name of our destination. He nodded and put our bags in his car and drove us to our hotel in Hellerton. At the desk we found our room reservations and followed a bellboy to the elevator.

Returning to the lobby, we were surprised to find Jens waiting for us. After much handshaking he said, "I have my car and will take you wherever you like to go. You will eat the evening meal with us."

"You are a student here and live near the university?" I asked.

"Yes, I go to the university, but Ilga and I and our little boy live in an apartment. She is working in the daytime. She will come home in the evening and we will have dinner together."

I knew he was not married. To meet this girl he was living with—would I be shocked? Worse than that, would I embarrass him by the expression on my face? Carefully I squirmed out of the dinner invitation, giving excuses.

Jens took us to the wharf, to see the little mermaid, to watch the hydrofoil take off for Sweden, to Elsinore castle where Hamlet was supposed to have lived. At noon he stopped the car at the curb on a street in the heart of the town.

"This is where we live," he said. "You will come in, please. We will eat our lunch here. Ilga has it placed on the table."

We went down three steps and entered an apartment just below the ground surface. The simple furnishings—the clean white curtains, the rows of books, the table spread for three—calmed my ruffled emotions.

"Ilga eats near her work," he said as he seated us. "Our little boy attends a nursery."

He heated the soup and served it with many kinds of cheese and bread, then little Danish cakes and dark coffee.

All afternoon we went sight-seeing about the town. Dropping us at our hotel at five o'clock, he said, "And now Ilga and I will return later and we will go to Tivoli together."

I looked up quickly.

"I have explained to your husband," he said to me. "It is the entertainment center of Kobenhaven. You will like it."

At eight o'clock Jens came again, leading us to his car. With no embarrassment he introduced us to the charming young woman who sat in the back. He helped me onto the seat beside her. She smiled and greeted me.

"Ilga and I will marry when I finish medical school. We do not have the money now. Income taxes are very high for married couples, not so for unmarried ones."

There was no apologizing tone in his voice. He was just explaining an accepted custom of their country. Keeping the fixed smile on my face, I thought rapidly: Don't let your consternation show in your face or your voice. You have no right to criticize Jens.

Tivoli is a gay place. Our evening was a gala experience. Curious Chinese pagodas were brightly lighted and reflected in a lake beside them. There were outdoor cafes, where we ate strange foods, and many entertainment spots. We went through the room of mirrors, laughing at our grotesque reflections.

After we told Jens and Ilga good-bye at the hotel and they had gone, Wendell turned to me.

"You masqueraded very well," he said. "I was afraid your Puritan scruples would stick out all over you like porcupine quills." And he laughed.

"I'm learning," I said.

The Spanish Boy
Who Gave His Life for a Teacher

"If I had been there, I could have been the English teacher," I told my husband when I came home from college that evening.

"But you were not there. You were in a plane flying over the Atlantic Ocean," he answered. "Aren't you glad you decided to ask the dean for permission to go with me to Rome on that business trip?"

"What a traumatic experience it would have been!" I said and shuddered.

Our college was located in the part of the city where interracial struggles ran rampant at times. When we taught night classes, we often found the police standing at the front door of the college building waiting to escort us to our cars when we were ready to go home. Our parking lot was across the street, and we had to ascend a long flight of steps to the dark, unlighted, gloomy spot.

The night dean had acted as a part-time policeman for several years when he was an instructor. He still kept his loaded revolver in his desk drawer in the office.

One evening two students came running to the front office, their eyes wide with fear.

"There's a man in the girls' rest room," they stammered, almost incoherently, "and he's showing himself and trying to grab the girls!"

"Which room?" the dean barked.

"Second floor!"

As they answered him, he was reaching into the drawer and pulling out the gun. He was out of the office and starting up the front stairs in a moment. He pounded down the hall, swung open the door of the rest room—it was empty. Turning his head he saw a man disappearing around the corner, away down the hall and to the back stairs. In a moment the dean was running down the steps. When he reached the back door he saw the figure of a man disappearing into a clump of bushes on the far side of the campus. He raced across the open, beat through the bushes, but found no sign of the intruder.

Returning to the college, he reported to the police. They came and searched the vicinity carefully for an hour or more. No results!

Another time two girls, leaving the college after night classes, walked out the main door and across the street. They carried their notebooks and books on one arm, and dangled their purses from the other. Suddenly they felt their purses grabbed, a hand held tightly over their mouths.

"If you scream, we'll kill you," one fellow said.

The assailants cut the purse straps, ran quickly down the streets. The girls, returning to the college, told of their loss; the police came—no success!

One afternoon one of the other English teachers went to the faculty parking lot, got into her car, and carefully locked the doors from the inside. She drove her car out into the street. Two big fellows climbed onto her car, demanding that she open the car doors and let them in or they would shoot her.

Very much frightened, not knowing what to do, she drove quickly toward the main street where the great number of cars and people must have intimidated the two young hoodlums who slipped off the car and were soon lost to view.

Always when I went to my car at night, I opened both front and back doors and searched between the seats for possible hidden molesters before I got into the driver's seat and locked all the doors. Once on my way home as I drove through a part of the city that was notorious for its uprisings, I was stopped at an intersection traffic light. Three burly young fellows stood in front of my car, demanding that I open my car door. I just sat there, engine running, so scared I couldn't breathe. Then a surge of traffic arrived and the three fellows disappeared.

Fortunately I was not there the night a real tragedy occurred.

The English teacher whose room was just next to mine had classes also until nine thirty at night. After her last class was dismissed and the students gone, she gathered her books and papers and laid them carefully in her briefcase, turned out the room lights, and went wearily down the front stairs. The night dean stood in the hall near the front office.

"Good-night," he called to her.

She answered, "Good-night," and pulled open the heavy front door and went across the street. She climbed the steps to the parking lot and started toward her car. Suddenly a young man stepped out from behind a parked car and yelled, "Give me your pocketbook!"

She saw the revolver in his right hand. He reached for her purse. At that moment a student who must have been close by pushed in between the bandit and the teacher.

"You let my teacher be," he called in broken Spanish-English.

"Get out of the way," the ruffian shouted, waving his gun.

Without waiting for the order to be obeyed he shot three times—directly at the student who staggered, then dropped to the ground. Alarmed, the assailant loosed his hold on the purse and ran.

The teacher dropped to her knees beside the twitching boy and screamed for help. "Felipe, it is you! Oh, I'm so sorry!"

The dean came quickly, followed by a policeman, but it was too late.

"Who is it? What happened?"

"His name is Felipe Cassandro, a Cuban refugee. He attends my evening class. He tried to defend me. He saved my life, but . . ." She was crying and stammering, almost in hysteria.

The boy died in the ambulance on the way to the hospital.

But the thought stays always with me: I might have been the English teacher if I had not been winging my way across the Atlantic that night, sitting safely beside my husband.

A Bonus

Betty Rheims was older than the others in the class. I did not notice this the first few weeks, but her essays told me.

"I have been out of school for seventeen years," she wrote, "and I am scared of college. But I want to try to do the work here. I have not given up my job and if I don't make passing grades I'll quit college. I am taking just two courses."

She sat near the back of the classroom during that first semester and was hesitant about offering her opinion in a discussion. Her essays had many mechanical errors, misspelled words, singular verbs with plural subjects, sentence fragments. But she expressed herself in good, strongly worded statements. Her thinking was good. After a few weeks she began to stop after class now and then and ask questions.

"You say, 'No thesis sentence.' What's a thesis? Why have one?"

I explained and then referred her to pages of her text.

"You wrote in the margin of my paper 'ambiguity.' What's that mean? I looked up the word in the dictionary and I still don't quite understand. But I want to learn how to correct my essay."

Very slowly her writing improved, but there was so much for her to learn. After mid-term exams, she was discouraged

189

with the D in English. She stopped in at my office to ask if she should drop the course.

I looked into her eyes and watched them brim with tears. She turned her head to hide the show of emotion.

"No," I said. "In the first place quarter grades are not recorded permanently. They are just warnings. You are progressing. Not as fast as you'd like to, but you'll make a C by the end of the semester. Why not sit down and talk to me a bit?"

She laid her books on a corner of my desk and dropped into the chair nearby.

"I went to work before I had finished high school," she explained. "I earned my own expenses that last year and then went right on working. It's not much of a job. For the last year or two I have been bored with my work. There's no thinking required. There's no possibility of advancement. The more I've thought about it, the more determined I have become to try to improve myself. This past summer I puzzled what to do.

"In July I came to the college here, talked with a counselor, and took the entrance tests. My scores weren't high, but he encouraged me to enroll in some college courses. I registered for two subjects."

"The other course," I said, "are you doing okay there?"

"Yes, it's history—one of those regurgitation classes— read, memorize, check true or false on an objective test. I can do that easily. But this composition course includes so many things I either didn't learn in school or else have forgotten."

"That's true. But don't you find that you are getting hold of some of this each week?"

"I learn a few things, but I then find a few hundred more things to learn." She smiled a little quirky grimace.

"What are you planning as a major?" I asked.

"Elementary Education," she said eagerly. "I think it has been in the back of my mind for years. I have never married, as you can see by my name, but I enjoy children. In my church school I teach kindergarten or primary classes. I like youngsters that age best and seem to relate to them."

"That's great! The most important instructor in a child's education is the one who teaches his first grade reading. She builds a bridge for the rest of his learning process and sets a pattern for his attitudes, his ability to take facts from a printed page and assimilate them in his mind. It's a wonderful but awesome goal!"

She nodded her head. "But if I can't get English—and it is a required course—then I should face the fact realistically and try to be satisfied with my present job."

"Well, let's give it a few more weeks of trial before you withdraw. Talk to me again before you go to the registrar, will you?"

She promised. Her improvement was gradual, but it was sure. Each new point of rhetoric she mastered was added permanently to her skills. At the end of the semester, she had a C—a good average college grade, as I so often tell the students to explain to their unbelieving parents who expect such miracles from their children.

During the second semester she sat near the front of the classroom, and her comments—especially when we discussed difficult reading assignments—were more mature, more profound than those of the younger students. I could see the admiration of the class for Betty when she aptly "tied up" a rambling, unfocused discussion with a pointed remark.

In the spring near the end of the semester, she came to my office to talk about an assigned research paper.

"Are you taking any college classes this summer?" I asked.

"No, but I do want to enroll in more courses in September," she said. "Could you give me any advice on what subjects to take?"

"Well, you must keep in mind the requirements for pre-education curriculum. But another good beginning subject I would suggest is the introduction to literature class. It would be a basic for the children's reading course which you will be taking later."

"Of course, I may not have enough money saved by September so I can pay my tuition and buy my books. I must face this."

"Have you looked into the grants and scholarships that are available, especially those offered students who want to major in elementary education?"

"No. How do I do this?"

We talked of her making an appointment with a counselor, of the questions she should ask him, and of government loans.

"Now, if none of these fits your case, and you don't have enough money, I'll pay your tuition," I offered.

She drew back. "I wasn't asking for charity," she said.

I put out my hand to touch her. "It wouldn't be charity; it would be an investment."

"But if I couldn't pay you back?"

"I call it an investment in people, in the future, in the citizens of the nation. I've done it for a number of students. I think you will make a good teacher. It gives me a great deal of satisfaction. You wouldn't deny me that, would you?"

"Well . . . I'll try these other things first." She stood up and began to collect her books and papers. "Thank you."

"Anyway write down my telephone number and let me know."

Often during the summer I thought of her. Once I even

went to the telephone and called the registrar to get her address and phone number. I hesitated at the telephone, tempted to call her. But I knew I should give her time to do what she could on her own.

One evening in late August I answered the telephone. "This is Betty Rheims," a voice said.

"I'm so glad to hear from you. I've wondered how you were doing. Are you registered for the fall semester?"

"Yes. I want to tell you all about it. I waited until I was sure before I called you. Just yesterday I had the final notice that a government loan had been granted to me. It is enough for all my tuition and books. After I graduate, if I teach school, each year a certain amount of the loan will be subtracted from the principal of the loan. It's great, isn't it?"

"You bet!" I shouted.

"And if I make good grades this year, I have been promised a scholarship that will make it possible for me to stop my job and go to college full time. But the best thing about it all was your confidence in me. All summer I'd say to myself, 'I *am* going to college. If I don't have the money, Mrs. Townsend will help me.' And I was not afraid to talk to the counselor. Now I am sure I will get an education and become a teacher."

"I knew you could do it—and you proved that you could do this thing by yourself," I answered.

"But always there was your faith in me that gave me the courage to keep calling and investigating. If *you* thought I could do it, then I knew I could."

"It's so good to hear you say this," I said lamely. "I'll see you in September."

The salary of the teacher is only a fraction of the remuneration that she gets from her profession. The other pay can't be measured in dollars and cents.

In the Wheelchair

From my students I have learned many things. This student gave me a marvelous lesson in humility.

It was in a class in English composition, a required course, that I met him. Most of the students in this group were boys of about seventeen years of age. As I began the first morning of the semester I said to them with a broad grin, "How many of you don't like English?"

A few hands popped up.

"Come on, now. I'm not grading you on this."

Many more students raised their hands. I laughed aloud and they turned to grin at each other.

"Okay," I said and they dropped their arms. "This is a real challenge to me. I hope somehow in this semester to make English interesting or at least to show you how necessary it is for you to have a working knowledge of your own language."

One student who had not raised his hand sat in a wheelchair near my desk. He was a big fellow, his shoulders slumped over. On his apparently immobile feet were piled books and notebooks. On his lap lay the two texts for this course. A wide rubber band which circled the back of his head made secure the thick eyeglasses he wore. But his eyes were very bright, and he seemed to be keenly aware of what was transpiring in the room.

As the class period progressed, the other students began to take notes. A fellow sitting in a desk near the wheelchair leaned over to whisper to the occupant, then took a ball-point pen out of the latter's pocket, placed it in his right hand and opened a notebook on his lap.

A few days later one of the college counselors called me to his office.

"Mrs. Townsend, I have been wanting to talk to you. I believe you have Ben Burson in your eight o'clock class."

"Burson, Burson?" I said puckering the skin above my nose.

"In a wheelchair!"

"I have three students in wheelchairs in that class."

"This fellow is completely helpless, can't even lift his arms."

"Oh, yes!"

The counselor pointed to a folder on his desk.

"This is Burson's cumulative record. I want to tell you something about him. His father called us this summer about the possibility of his son's attending Junior College. He explained that Ben has had a gradual paralysis of his entire body, beginning with his toes. For most of his life he has been becoming more paralyzed. At present he can move only parts of his face and the ends of his fingers."

I must have made some sound of empathy for the counselor paused a moment and then proceeded.

"His doctor talked to me over the phone. The young fellow has only six months to a year to live. On purpose I put him in your class. I was sure you'd understand. Would you like to look over his records?"

I sat for a while leafing through grade school teacher's comments and high school test scores, my emotions turmoiling.

Very early the next morning I happened to look out my office window and saw below me a delivery truck pulling up at the second basement entrance. On the panel of the truck I read "Larsens—Florists." A man got out of the front seat, walked to the back end of the truck, and opened the rear end double door. He lowered a slanting board and slowly edged a wheelchair to the concrete driveway. In the chair I saw Ben Burson.

A little later as I hurried toward my classroom I passed the elevator and met this student in his wheelchair, being pushed out of the elevator cubicle and down the hall.

"Good morning," I said.

"Oh, Mrs. Townsend, I'd like for you to meet my father," said Ben.

The wheelchair was halted while the older man paused to shake hands with me. We moved on together. In the classroom, the older Mr. Burson reached under his son's armpits, lifted and tugged the helpless body into a more upright position, pulled the sagging shoulders against the chair back, pushed back the spectacles against the nose ridge, then laid a hand lovingly on his son's shoulders.

"Be back as soon as I can," he said and went back down the hall.

When the bell sounded I began the classwork, trying to keep my thoughts on English instead of Ben Burson.

Picking up a long piece of chalk I said, "You already know that the assignment for today is an essay written here in class. While I write several subjects on the blackboard, one of you fellows in the front row pass out that lined paper lying there on my desk."

As I wrote I talked of the topics I had chosen, trying to "build a fire," as I called it, under their imaginations. One by one the students got ideas and began to write. I helped Ben get his pen in his hand and his paper placed. The room was quiet except for the scratch of ball-point pens and the flip of papers. At the end of the hour everyone had completed his essay except Ben.

"Do you have a class next hour?" I said to him.

"No, not until ten o'clock."

"Would it be all right if I have someone bring you down to the second floor and to the hall near my office so that you can finish your writing there?"

"Fine, thank you!" he said slowly.

I left my office door open and now and then called out to him, asking him if he needed a word spelled or more paper.

The next day, as I read the essays from that class, I came to the theme written by Ben Burson. His handwriting was large and sprawling, but legible, the letters almost square-shaped in form. From the first sentence, I read with fascination. Parts of it struck my mind forcibly, tore at my sympathy.

"College is such a wonderful place. . . . People said I would not like it . . . that students would be cold and unfeeling. I have been so happy here. My classmates are all kind to me . . . so thoughtful. . . ." And then followed concrete illustrations with details of colorful imagery.

I was stunned. How many times I had passed him in his wheelchair, waiting passively for his father. Usually I had hurried by, only calling out a few words of greeting. Students had rushed past, even brushing against the wheelchair, seldom noticing the boy sitting there.

He can't even brush off a fly or wipe the sweat from his face, I had thought and winced.

Now, holding his essay before me, I looked out the window and thought of my own petty little grievances and pretended martyrdoms and felt ashamed. I wandered into the office of another English teacher to share the sentiments of this paper. Later I took a long time to write a note at the bottom of Ben's essay.

The next day as I passed out the corrected papers I said, "The grade is at the end of the essay. But more important than that are the comments I have written in the margins and on the last page. Don't ignore these."

Carefully I watched for Ben's reaction when he read his paper. Slowly he perused the pages, awkwardly sliding one page from the others, then raised his eyes to gaze straight into mine. I was satisfied. We had communicated.

The class period was taken up by a discussion of an assigned reading. By now the rapport of student-to-student and student-to-teacher had been established. The comments came fast and arguments became lively, sometimes heated.

"Mr. Burson," I said, "just speak out if you want to join the fray. Since you can't raise your hand, don't wait for me to call on you."

It was through Ben's written work that I discovered his interest in sports, especially baseball. He knew each player on all the well-known teams, the batting average, the number of bases stolen, the shutout games pitched. His prized possession was a remote-control button for his TV set at home, one so sensitive that his almost nerveless fingers could give the gentle pressure needed to change channels.

"No one needs to wait on me for that," he said.

On the last day of school before Christmas holidays Ben's father rapped on the office door. When I called out "Come in," I was surprised to see a great sheaf of flowers coming through the doorway, hiding a man's face and shoulders.

I gasped out something.

"From Ben to you," he said as he stood holding out the

enormous bouquet of long-stemmed pink snapdragons.

"Oh, you shouldn't have—"

"It's okay. I work for a florist. When I want I can have flowers. It's the only way I know to say thanks for your interest in my son. He is so happy in your class."

My arms full of the flowers, I stood there, completely speechless. "Ben is a fine student," I said finally. "His mind is good; his thinking is straight and true."

"Well, you see, he wanted to come to college, wanted it more than anything. Our neighbors and friends think we are crazy."

"It isn't easy for you, bringing him here and coming to get him besides doing your regular work."

"We don't mind the inconvenience or the extra work. You see we love him, his mother and I. We know he won't be with us much longer. We want him to enjoy every moment of this time."

He paused and looked at me to see whether I understood.

"Well, I've got to go to work," he said.

Inadequately I thanked him as he left the room.

Later in the morning another instructor, coming into my office, saw the flowers.

"Hey! Where'd you get that enormous bouquet? A birthday?" she called out.

"From a student!"

"What! Don't you know we are not supposed to accept gifts—bribes—from students?"

Instantly I was furious. "I must accept these," I returned sharply. "I can't refuse." And then, calming down, I told of the student.

Unconvinced she left the office, shaking her head in negation.

The second semester I had Ben in a literature class. He

read avidly, seeming to understand the motives, identifying with a wide variety of characters and situations. That fall I did not see him except occasionally in the hall. He was in none of my classes. But when I stopped to chat with him as he waited in his wheelchair, he seemed unchanged.

One day Miss Adams came to my office and after a few amenities said, "Elsie, why weren't you at Ben Burson's funeral this morning? You knew him quite well, didn't you?"

"Oh, yes! But I didn't know!"

"Yes, he died Saturday night. The office called me about it. I had him in class Friday."

"I wonder why I wasn't told."

"Don't you have him in a class?"

"Not this semester."

"That's probably it. Your name wasn't on his present course card. Anyway, after the service for Ben, I went to speak to his father. As soon as I said I was from Junior College, he asked, 'But why isn't Mrs. Townsend here? I was sure she'd be here.' "

For a second I covered my eyes. "I'm so sorry I wasn't told."

After the other teacher had left, I picked up a pen, hunted for a clean page of paper, and began struggling with words to form a message to Ben's parents. Again and again I scratched out sentences, words. How could I tell them the sorrow and yet the peace in my heart?

Phrases began to form themselves—"You must know that your son is free at last . . . released from the prison of his body . . . is no longer . . . chained to a wheelchair. . . . His mind, which ever soared, can keep on soaring. . . ."

I wrote and rewrote. I sent the note. But in my life remained the vivid picture of this student who taught me a new lesson in humility.

Game Playing

Usually I am proud of being a teacher. I like the old quotation, "And gladly wolde he learn and gladly teche." I think of it as of a profession, an altruistic service. But dreadful deeds have been perpetrated in the name of teaching.

One afternoon as I collected the papers on my desk and stowed them into my briefcase, I looked up to see Don Readwell at the open door of the office. His face was flushed, his eyes angry, and his whole body was rigid.

"Can I come in? You're alone, Mrs. Townsend? Can I close the door?" he said with no pause.

He did not wait for my answer. When he had shut the door with a bang, he strode past me to the window and began to pour out a string of swear words, maledictions, ominous predictions—the words almost unintelligible in their rapid utterance. He punctuated his expressions by striking the metal filing cabinet with his fist occasionally. For a minute or more this continued; then he dropped into the chair near the window.

I swiveled my chair around so that I could look at him directly.

"I'm sorry for my tirade, Mrs. Townsend, but I had to get rid of that or explode. I knew you'd let me blow off."

"What in the world is this all about?" I asked.

"It's that English class!"

"But I don't have you in any of my classes, do I? You were in English 101 last semester."

"That's right! But you know me, and I had to come to someone who would understand. Right now I am taking English 102 from Miss Stinger—couldn't arrange my schedule so I could get into your class. You know her, don't you? She's a --" and he again went into a paroxysm of profanity and obscenity.

"But tell me your problem. Are you having difficulty with the course?"

"It's my essays. She just hands 'em back with a D or an F on them—no comments."

"But you made good grades in English composition. You can express yourself very aptly. What is the matter?"

"Oh, it's not the mechanics. I asked her that. She said, 'No!' Then I asked her how I could improve and she said I must discover that myself. How can I do that when I don't know what to change?"

"Do you disagree with what she believes? Her moral values? Her ideas of present problems?"

"I don't know. I can't tell what she thinks. But it just goes on and on. And here's the crux of the problem. I have been accepted in premed at the University for the fall semester. Now you know that two semesters of English composition are still required, and the grades must be C or above or they are not accepted."

"How are your grades in the other courses you're taking?"

"Good! Got an A in anthropology, B in chemistry, A in psychology. But look what a D or an F would do to my record."

"Have you talked with a counselor?"

202

"No—it's just my word against a teacher's. I'd never get anywhere there."

"Well, I know one counselor who used to be an English teacher. Why not go to see him? Perhaps he'll understand and will suggest what to do."

I talked of an appointment, gave the name of the counselor, and explained the location of his office.

"Let me know what success you have."

He picked up his notebooks and texts, then paused for a few parting shots. "Of all the mean sergeants I have ever known, she beats them all. I thought when I got away from the injustices of Army discipline . . ." And he opened the door and went away.

I watched him leave and sat thinking of his life—what I knew of it. I knew he was in his late twenties, a diligent student—not rebellious—a conscientious husband, a loyal soldier. But now he felt thwarted in his desire to study in a profession—to improve his mind—to complete a dream he had been preparing for and thinking about for many years. He was completely baffled—like a rat in a complex maze.

In a few days he came again, this time not explosive, just defeated. He dropped limply into the chair by my desk.

"What did the counselor say?" I asked hesitantly.

"Told me I was too full of pride. Said I must abase myself—knuckle under. Now, just how do I abase myself? I'd be willing to crawl up the steps of the Washington Monument on my knees if I could get a grade with that teacher. I'd even stoop to brownnosing if I knew what to do."

"I know this is highly unethical," I said slowly, "but flattery works sometimes where anger and contradiction fail. Let's plan a strategy to win this woman to your side. I know a few points where teachers are sensitive. And I do know this teacher. Try a little apple-polishing—not too heavy-handed or she will catch on. Stop after class and comment on the interesting conclusions that she brought out in the discussion of the hour. Agree with her on some moot point she has made. Keep your fingers crossed behind you, if it helps."

I turned to look at him. "Can you be meek?"

He grinned wryly. "To get a grade on my transcript I would do anything but out and out cheat."

"Think up nice things to say. Look for something specific, but be sure it will agree with her opinions. She holds the whip I know. Wasn't it Franklin who said that a small amount of honey will catch more flies than a jug of vinegar?"

He nodded, his eyes vague with thoughts going on inside his head.

I continued. "Plan a strategy of attack. Write what you know would please her, concepts that you know she would agree with. Use her ideas, only rephrase them in some way. Play them back to her—but subtly—softly—softly."

There was almost a smug sneer on his face.

"No," I said quickly, "not satirically. Save that for some future day. Will you try my tactics?"

He nodded.

"I feel pretty sneaky," I admitted, "but I had to use this method on a professor I had in a graduate school literature couse. He said, 'Express your opinions.' I did and got a C on my first essay. After that I reflected his ideas and got all A's."

We grinned like conspirators as he left my office.

I did not see him again. In June I looked at his records in the registrar's office. My finger traced down the list of credits until I came to English 102—B. Feeling only a little guilty, I left the office.

Make Your Own Opportunity

One of the common excuses we hear from people is this one: "Oh, I never did get to go to college. We were poor, couldn't afford it." When I hear this I shrivel a little, but then my thoughts go quickly to one family I knew at Junior College—the Stockings.

I met Mrs. Stocking first. She was in my second semester English class. I noticed her waiting in the front lobby each evening as I started to go home. The class of mine that she was in was a late one. After its dismissal, every student scurried out of the room, hurried to lockers, banged them with a finality of end-of-day conclusion, and left the building. The halls were deserted in a few minutes—except for Mrs. Stocking, who leaned against one of the front doors and waited. Out of sheer curiosity I stopped to question her one evening.

"Oh, I'm waiting for my husband," she said. "He'll be here as soon as he can."

"Where does he work?"

"He's a teacher in the high school at_____" and she named a town almost twenty miles distant, but in the same direction that I lived.

"Could I give you a ride some evening as far as the shopping center near 40 Highway? It's right on my way and I could save your husband at least twenty miles of driving."

"I'll talk to him tonight and maybe we could make arrangements. He comes that way."

She thanked me, and I picked up my heavy briefcase and started out the door.

Two days later, after class, she stayed in the room after the class had poured out into the hall.

"My husband said he'd be waiting where you turn off Highway 40 and go onto Crysler Street. This isn't out of your way, is it?"

"No, I go that route every evening."

I went to my office, collected a pile of English themes to check, and met her at the front door. As we traveled together, we talked of her family.

"How come you're over here at Junior College?" I asked. It is always interesting to know why a woman of about forty or more decides to begin college.

"Well, my husband insisted. You see, he found college so interesting. Just a year ago last spring he graduated from the university. But he began at Junior College. It was Mr. Grundy in the commercial department who asked him why he didn't come here and take college courses.

" 'But I never even finished high school,' my husband told him. 'Then you can take the government exam and if you make a high enough score you are eligible for day school. Even if your score is low, you can begin with evening classes.'

"My husband thought about it, mainly because his job was so lacking in a future. The pay was low, and not enough for us to live on. I was working in a laundry, getting seventy-five cents an hour. Jack, our son, was ten years old."

She paused and I urged her on.

"You see, my husband and I grew up in the southern part of the state. I had only had two years of high school when we married; I was young. He became a sort of traveling preacher for a religion that was only local. And then, after a few years, it just sort of folded up. We had no income, no trade, no profession. We came here to the city, worked at anything we could get. It was tough sledding most of the time.

"Well, four years ago, when we met Mr. Grundy at a church social we were so completely discouraged—ready to try anything.

"Jim—that's my husband—promised to try the test. Mr. Grundy made an appointment for him with the counselor at Junior College, even came to take him there. The counselor telephoned when he had the results of the GED test; wanted Jim to come to the college to see the scores and have them explained. That night when my husband came home he just walked in the door, came over to me, put his arms around me and held me tight. He couldn't talk at first.

"After a while he explained, 'My scores are good. I've been accepted as a student, come September. I don't know how we can do it, but if I get a night job Mr. Grundy offered to pay the tuition. It sounds like a dream. Are you willing to try?'"

I turned from my driving to glance at her. Her eyes were bright with tears but she was smiling. She began to talk again.

"I kept on at the laundry. Jim found a night job—not good, but it would do. Our little son was in school during the day. Jim was home on Saturdays when I was gone. He didn't get much sleep, just studied and worked. His first few weeks at college were tough. He received terrible grades in English because he didn't have the necessary high school background. When the marks on his essays were D's, his eyes had the look of a wounded animal. But he never once talked of giving up.

"Once I asked him why not quit, and he said, 'But Mr. Grundy has confidence in me. I can't fail him!'

"Jim was halfway through his second year before he

decided his field would be education in social science. He wanted to be a high school teacher.

"When he graduated from Junior College he began to plan for his entrance into the university. His application for a government loan was granted. This would pay for his tuition and books. But he still would have to keep his forty-hour-a-week job and I would keep mine.

"During his fourth year, he began to correct my errors in speaking. There was talk about better clothes for me and for our son. I knew I had fallen behind him in education; sometimes I was too embarrassed to go with him to college functions.

"Just before he graduated in the spring, he came home one night and handed me a thick folded paper. 'Read it,' he said. 'It's a contract to teach in a high school about twenty-five miles east of here. Shall I sign? Would you like to drive out to see it before we decide?'

" 'Have you talked with Mr. Grundy?' I asked. 'He's been our best guide.'

" 'Mr. Grundy is the man who recommended me for the position. He drove me out there to meet members of the school board. I was so afraid that I wouldn't be offered a contract that I didn't tell you before.'

"The next Sunday we drove to the area and walked all around the school buildings. Jim signed the contract. On the way home he said, 'Now our next step is to get you enrolled in Junior College for this September.'

"That night I cried for a long time, whether from fear, anxiety, or joy I don't know—probably a mixture of all. During the summer we rented a little house not too far from the high school. There was space for a garden, a little pasture for a cow. In August we both quit our jobs and moved out there. I began to attend the college.

"We get up at four o'clock in the morning. Jim milks the cow while I get breakfast and pack our lunches. We drive over here to Junior College. Jim goes back to his school. Before the school bus picks up Junior, he puts the cow in the pasture and does the other chores. After school, Jim drives over here for me. We work pretty late, then study till about midnight. But we're making it, and we're so happy."

Mrs. Stocking continued to ride home with me for the remainder of the semester, meeting her husband at Crysler and 40 Highway. In May when we met him, he asked me to wait a moment. Coming to my car, he put in the back seat several gallons of freshly picked strawberries.

"We have a good crop," he said simply.

Graduation night a year later I was dawdling in the front hall taking off my gown and hood. I felt someone touch my shoulder and turned to face Mrs. Stocking.

"Oh, Mrs. Townsend, I just must share my joy with someone or I'll burst wide open."

When I smiled her eyes filled with tears.

"This is a wonderful night for us," she said. "I have my associate degree and have been accepted in the university for next fall. My husband graduated with his master's degree last night. And Junior will be in this college in September. And all because a commercial teacher talked to my husband six years ago."

"You had something to do with this, too," I said as I put my arm around her. "How proud you should be!"

Jim

Jim Zandee was a tall, spare young fellow who jackknifed his long body into a seat and under the desk in the back of the classroom. Immediately I judged his age at twenty-five at least. There were fine lines in his forehead, and a crease in each cheek.

When we began to discuss some passages we had read, he leaned forward, his head turning to look intently at each speaker. Interested, he seemed, yet he took no audible part. His eyes were vitally alive; the expressions on his face changed with the tenor of the discussion.

For a week or more I did not call on him, waiting for voluntary contribution. One day a student spoke derisively of chauvinistic flag-wavers in America. Instantly Jim Zandee's hand was in the air. He began to speak almost before I nodded at him.

"That remark makes me furious," he said. "I have just returned from a long stretch in the Navy, and I'll defend my country's position in the Pacific."

And he did, with ardor, succinctly and convincingly. His opponents quailed before his arguments which were filled with facts, exact details.

I took note of him, judging his logic, his attitude, his willingness to support a proposition that was being ridiculed constantly by the young college students. A few days later, as

I graded a stack of essays from this class, I found myself rereading the one written by Mr. Zandee. At the bottom of the paper I wrote, "Excellent. Are you interested in stopping at my office sometime? I'd like to talk it over with you?"

Very early the next morning he came, folding his length into the chair near my desk as I said, "Good morning! Up early?"

"No, just haven't yet gone to bed. Got off work at seven and came here directly."

"Where do you work?"

"At the post office downtown."

"Full time?"

"Yes, forty hours a week."

"And you carry a full load of college credits besides that?"

"Yes, I have a lot of catching up to do. You see I've been out of school for eight years. Enlisted in the Navy right after high school."

"What are you interested in? Have you chosen a major?"

"I suppose it will be languages, German perhaps, but what I'd really like to study is Chinese."

"How come?"

"Well, I was stationed much of my time at Okinawa. I got bored so I began to take some courses at the university there. I have thirty-two credits in Mandarin."

"Sounds fascinating. Why don't you go on with it?"

"Can't, I guess. I have talked to counselors, teachers. Nobody seems to think these credits are any good—no department of Chinese in the colleges around here."

I shook my head. "I don't know, but I'd like to find out. In the meantime for the research paper I have assigned later on why not write on some problem in the Chinese language?"

"A problem?"

"Something to be solved, to be proved, to be changed. Think about a thesis for this and let me know. And I'll scrounge around to see what I can find out about universities with departments in Chinese."

After he was gone, I went to the registrar's office.

"Will you give me a look at Jim Zandee's first semester credits?" I asked the girl at the desk.

She brought me a drawer of alphabetized cards which began with the R's. I thumbed through until I found his. "Chemistry A, physics A, German A, English 101 A," I recorded in my mind. "Wow, what a load!"

Handing the drawer to the girl, I thanked her absent-mindedly and started down the hall to the counselors' wing of the building. I passed the first two offices—"Good counselors," I said to myself, "but neither is the one who would take hold of this problem and worry it as a dog does an old bone."

Before the third office I paused.

"Mean as a wildcat," I said to myself, remembering my last encounter with her when she had vituperatively accused me of "babying" the freshmen. But I had read her articles in educational magazines. She knew her field well, wrote with erudition on various subjects. Besides, she had traveled widely in the Orient. I had discovered that when I had complimented her on a jewelled pin shaped like a dragon she had pinned to a dress lapel.

With trepidation I knocked gently on her door, waited for her sharp "Come," and went into the room.

"Dr. Henley, I have a problem that I'm sure you can solve. I want to find a college where there is a department of Chinese. Is there such?"

"Why?" she asked sharply.

"I have a student who . . ."

She cut me off with "Another of your sentimental concerns for your students, I suppose."

"I hope it's more than this."

I told her of Jim Zandee. "He's good. He has something to offer, I think. I don't want him to go to waste."

"I can look in all the college catalogs," she conceded.

I thanked her and went back to my office. But I was sure I had piqued her curiosity.

Several weeks later Jim Zandee brought in the rough draft of his research paper. As I read it through I became so excited about the information he had in the field, the skill with which he had developed his thesis that I took the manuscript to the counselor's office.

"Read this, please," I said, "and you'll see why I am so interested in this student."

I held out the papers, proud of the neat, fine handwriting. She took the essay and began to read, ignoring me.

That afternoon Dr. Henley came to my office.

"I'd like to meet this student," she said, waving the pages of manuscript.

"I'll bring him in, say—after early class tomorrow?"

She nodded.

"I've got her hooked," I murmured to myself as she disappeared down the hall.

It was several days later that Jim Zandee found me in my office again, came hurrying to my desk to say, "Mrs. Townsend, she's interested in my problem. She's found several universities where I can get a degree in the Chinese language. She is writing for particulars."

I nodded. He went on. "Besides, she wants a copy of my research paper—for herself."

"Tell me more as soon as you know."

It must have been three weeks before he stopped at my

office again. This time joy was written across his features.

"Dr. Henley wrote a letter recommending me to the head of the Chinese department in a college in_____, a good private college. She has had an answer—an offer to me of a thousand dollars a year scholarship."

"Whoopee!" I shouted.

"Wait! I have another problem. You remember I told you I am married. My wife works as a secretary. Dr. Henley is writing to find a job for my wife in an office of the college."

"Keep me informed," I said.

Another week went by. Then early one morning Jim met me at the front door of the college building.

"I've been waiting for you," he said. "It's all settled. My wife has a job in the office of the department of Chinese in the college where I have the scholarship. Fantastic, isn't it? We'll move to the town as soon as my classes here end. Already we're packing."

I saw him only once again after the semester ended. A year later, one summer afternoon, while I was showing some friends around the college building, I heard someone call my name. I turned to see a tall fellow running down the hall.

"What great luck!" he said. It was Jim Zandee. "You remember me, don't you?"

I nodded and reached out my hand.

"I never did get an opportunity to thank you," he said. "But what I wanted most to tell you is that it's been terrific. The university accepted all my credits from Okinawa at face value. I'll be a senior this fall. And I'm not going to stop with a bachelor's degree—all this because I happened to take a course from a little half-pint sized English teacher."

"Sounds good for my ego, but I can't take all the credit. Have you told Dr. Henley?"

"That's what I just did, and then I met you."

The White Black Woman

The room soon began to fill with students for the night class which began at eight o'clock and ended at nine-thirty. I started to collect the enrollment cards knowing that more students would trickle in as soon as they had located the room. In the hall outside the door, I heard students matching number on the course card with the number over the door: "Second floor, Room 206; yep, the right one!"

The rear seats having been taken by the early students, the front desks began to fill. I wrote my name on the blackboard, then stood at the lectern and glanced over the room—students of every age, of various colors, of all sizes. I enjoyed the night classes, except when I was too tired, because most of the students came to learn, not just to earn credits.

Through my mind ran part of a poem entitled "Noah's Ark." "The animals came in two by two—the elephant and the kangaroo. . . ."

But really this was the challenge of teaching—welding together heterogeneous individuals into a group, a real college class of learning. As usual the excitement of this challenge quickened my heartbeat and sent my blood pounding rapidly through my body.

Enunciating carefully, I began to read the names from the enrollment cards. The time moved slowly, as first sessions always did. Most of the students did not yet have their textbooks. In an hour I could feel the sag in attention. I looked at my watch.

"It's only nine o'clock, but I am going to dismiss you," I said. "Next time you will have read the assignments and you can do much of the talking."

As they picked up notebooks and briefcases, I began to collect my papers and books. One woman came to my desk and stood looking hesitantly at me.

"It's been so long since I was in school," she said. "I feel absolutely lost."

"You won't be in a few weeks. It's too early in the course to be worried about that. You'll catch on fast," I said and smiled up at her. "Ask questions. Don't be afraid that others will think you're dumb. Realize that they're wanting to know too, and are glad someone else stuck his neck out."

It was very dark where my car stood in the parking lot. I opened the door, switched on the overhead light and looked carefully all over the interior. Getting in under the steering wheel, I reached to lock the doors, and drove toward home.

After a few night sessions of this class, I became conscious of the tall woman in the front seat to my left. She was quick to give the right answers, asked intelligent questions. Often she came early, standing patiently in the hall outside until my six thirty class had been dismissed. When she laid her briefcase on that front desk and slid into the seat, she looked expectantly toward me, offering a quick smile for my "Good evening!"

Her hair was black, carefully arranged in curls and waves. She had large black eyes which seemed to take in everything and everyone. She wore simple cotton dresses which fitted her slender figure, and she walked with grace and dignity.

One night, when the course was about one-third completed, she stayed after the others had gone. Looking up at me she spoke, and her voice sounded strong in the quiet room.

"Mrs. Townsend, I don't think you realize that I'm Black!"

"Should I?" I asked.

"Yes!"

"Should it make any difference?"

"Well—anyway, you ought to know."

"Okay. Thank you for telling me."

There was nothing apologetic; it was just an act of communicating.

At the end of the quarter her exam grade was a B. Looking at her face I read the distress that she felt.

"It's just one grade," I hurried to explain. "I have many grades in my book for you, most of them A's. Besides, quarter grades are not permanently recorded. Only semester grades count. Give me time and I'll make an accurate estimate of what you can do."

The puckered lines between her eyes seemed to soften and her eyes looked directly at me as we went on with the classwork.

By the end of the term we had become good friends. She was always there early and there was often a short period of time between the classes. She told me of new recipes, southern dishes I had never known about, and I brought a slip of a climbing honeysuckle for her to take home and plant beside her trellis.

Then, one night, just before finals, she was absent from class. I missed her active participation. At the next session she came early, but she was very quiet. Her eyes looked at me, at the students speaking, but her thoughts seemed far from the discussion.

After class, I busied myself with erasing the writing I had made on the blackboard and filling my briefcase. She was still sitting there at her desk after all the other students had gone.

"Mrs. Townsend," she said, "I waited to talk to you. My son was married Monday."

She hesitated and looked down for a moment. I waited. Lifting her head high she went on, "And he married a white girl. This has been a traumatizing experience for me. I was furious. I was hurt. I was angry. My pride was torn and bleeding. Yes, I know he has none of the typical features of the Black and can easily pass as a White, but he had no right to do this to us—to his family."

I could not speak. Dazedly I was beginning to grasp her meaning—a surprising one for me.

"Mrs. Townsend, I found out that I had all sorts of prejudices that I didn't know I had."

I learned much that evening.

Ron Dutton

I noticed Ron Dutton immediately. He was so handsome, so clean looking. Very tall and slender, he stood erect. He had light curly hair and blue eyes. When he smiled, only one side of his lips turned up.

In a few weeks I recognized the rich background of reading that he had had, so much broader and deeper than any other student in the class. And his perception was lightning-quick. He was impatient with the plodding questions of slower students, with their lack of understanding.

When we began to read Pushkin's poetry, I discovered that Ron had studied Russian for two years. For pronunciation of the difficult names, I turned to him.

But he was restless, dissatisfied and critical. One afternoon he appeared at my office and stood in the doorway, the top of his head almost touching the top of the doorcase.

"Got a minute, Mrs. Townsend?" he asked.

Laying down my pen, I took off my glasses and rubbed my eyes.

"Wouldn't have to wear these darn things so that I could read if my arm was longer," I said. "Glad to quit these papers."

I motioned toward a chair. He folded his long torso and dropped into the seat.

"This man Rousseau! He's got me buffaloed! Why did he write all that tripe?"

And we were off on a lively discussion of "Candide." Soon we drifted to Ron's personal problems, his hangups.

"It's parents and teachers that bug me," he said. "They talk one thing and do just the opposite. Cripes! My folks think I shouldn't drink. And yet they tank up all the time. The refrigerator and the bar are full of liquor. What's with it in your generation?"

I laughed. "It takes all kinds, Ron," I mumbled inanely.

"Sure, Mom took me to church and left me there—came back later to get me. She and Dad didn't go—only kids need religion! Why? I don't get it! They preach to us about cheatin' but you ought to see my old man wrestle with the income tax forms—chiseling out every dime he won't get caught taking, lying a little here, conniving. I'm fed up with the whole farce. I think I'm going to join the Service. Uncle can't be any bigger hoax than my folks are. Sure they say, 'You gotta have a college degree. Everybody who is anybody goes to college.' "

By this time I had found my wits enough to shift the conversation a bit.

"What are you taking besides this course in world literature that I am teaching, Ron?"

We talked of required subjects, possible majors, future classes.

Ron's papers for the first exam did not surprise me, but they delighted me. His concepts of the purposes of the writers and their success in achieving or failing were mature thinking. His criticisms were sharp, but supported by accurate, forceful detail. When I handed back the test papers, he glanced at the grade, hid his exam in a notebook, and looked out the window self-consciously. Then he slipped the pages out again to read my comments in the margins. Once I caught his glance, and he smiled knowingly.

Near the end of the semester he stopped by my office door and said, "Knock, knock!" I looked up.

"Hey! Thought you might be interested. I'm going to the Navy soon as this semester ends—into their reserve program. Maybe during the time I spend there I will gain the perspective I need to be able to decide what I should do—go to college, get a job, or just go a-bumming."

He grinned, waved, and was gone.

A year passed. Second semester registration was almost over when I saw him again.

"I'm back," he said pulling up a chair opposite my place at the registration tables.

"Completed your hitch in the Service?"

"Yeah! Still on reserve though."

"What subjects have you listed on those course cards?"

He handed me the whole packet.

"No, not my mythology class!" I protested. "It's too easy for you."

"Only course you're teaching that I haven't taken already."

"But you've read most of the material of the texts. It's too elementary for you."

"I'll settle for a soft A," he said.

"But I don't want you spinning your wheels."

"You won't refuse to let me into the class, will you?"

"No, but I hate to see you bored."

He went on down the line of tables.

After a week of classes, Ron appeared at my office one afternoon.

"I read both of the texts of the course. Have you some more books on mythology that I might borrow?"

I turned to my bookshelves. "Help yourself," I offered, pointing to one particular shelf. He did. I think by actual count he read at least fourteen other books from my shelves. One day, at the end of class, I said to Ron, "Can you stay a few minutes after the class has gone?"

He nodded. After the students had filed out, he came to a student's desk near mine and slid into it.

"Would you be interested in a directed reading course? You could add it to your schedule. You need something to challenge you."

"What's it like?"

"You have an adviser—an English teacher in this case—and he directs your reading. You meet your adviser about once a week, discuss your interpretations of what you have read, make literary criticisms, do quite a bit of research, and perhaps write a paper."

"Sounds good! What do I read?"

"You choose—of course with the consent of your adviser. Is there some writer that interests you particularly? Or is there a literary period or theme?"

"Couldn't say right off. Can I think about it?"

"You should add it by tomorrow—that late registration restriction, you know."

The next morning, before my first class, he came into my office.

"Early bird, eh?" he said with his lopsided grin. He dropped into the chair near my desk.

"What did you decide?" I asked.

"Yeah! I think I'll take a crack at it."

"And your choice of reading?"

He hesitated and scratched his head a moment.

"You won't laugh?" he said quickly.

"Should I?"

"Well, it's Shakespeare. That guy bugs me. When I was in high school that old lady Barnes made reading Julius Caesar seem like months of prison sentence. But last winter I read through a couple of his plays. That old guy really says something now and then. I'd like to do a little digging in his writing."

"That's good! Now to get an adviser for you."

"Can't you be my adviser?"

"No, what with being head of the department and teaching a full load, I can't find the time. Besides Shakespeare's subtleties sometimes elude me. I think I could talk Dr. Gaston into taking you for a pupil. His research for his doctor's dissertation was in drama. He's deep! Okay?"

"If you say so."

"I'll go to see if I can find him right now, before we get snowed with students coming in."

The next day I did not see Ron until the afternoon. Mythology was my last class of the day. I saw him sitting in the back of the room listening to some lecture material I had for the hour. It was a large class, the chairs all full. At the end of the hour, I piled my texts and notebook in a stack and scooped them into my arms. In my office I found Ron waiting by my desk. I let the books slide out of my arms onto my desk and wearily pulled out my office chair.

"Last one of the day!" I growled. "Wow! Every one of my classes is loaded to the handlebars. I counted my registration lists and found that I have one hundred and ninety students. I'll never even learn their names."

Then I turned to Ron. "Just as I told you, Ron, this mythology class is too easy for you. Why don't you just challenge the course? I could give you a special project and you needn't even attend class."

"I don't want to miss the class discussion. I like that."

"That was a wild argument you and Jim Johnson had about Cronus and Zeus today." Most of the other students didn't even know what you were talking about. I felt like a referee in a free-for-all."

He laughed. "About that reading course you talked me into. I started in with *King Lear*. That Shakespeare constantly surprises me. He's deep! What would you say is the purpose of the play?"

I mumbled a few ideas—"On the surface the author is saying . . ."

"Yeah, but deeper than that! Wow, was I surprised at all the innuendoes of meaning we've been finding in that play!"

"Have you looked into the writings of some literary critics?"

"Found a few in the library. But I disagree with some of them—especially the older ones. Say, have you any?"

"I'll bring you some of my own. I like Van Doren."

The semester was over and the final exam week almost concluded when I had the last discussion with Ron.

"Busy, Mrs. T.?" he said as he dipped his head to come through the doorway of my office.

"I should be, but I'm not eager to tackle these finals. Come on in, Ron."

"Just that I might not get to see you again."

"Will you be with us another semester?"

"Nope, guess not. I'm going to the university this fall."

"And you'll be taking what?"

His crooked smile appeared and then disappeared before he answered.

"Literature, I guess. It really turns me on. Lots of the courses there at the university sound good to me. I want to take a crack at them. Don't know what I'll end up doing or being, but I'm not worrying about that right now."

"And I'll not be worrying about it either, Ron. You'll be okay."

224

I Learn from a Hippie

He walked into my class that first day with all the arrogance of a Great Dane. In the center of the room he dropped into a seat, kicked off his loose sandals, and lifted his dirty bare feet to the top of the desk ahead of him.

He saw me glaring at him. When I shook my head and frowned, he lowered his feet to the seat of the other desk, sliding his spine down until his huge bushy head rested on the back of his chair.

I stood there seething with repugnance. He insulted me with his appearance. Dirty uncombed hair hung to his shoulders. A straggly beard hid much of his face. His unwashed shirt of flowered material had been deliberately chopped and fringed at the bottom and above the elbows. Just below the knees his tattered jeans showed the same results of scissors clippings.

"I'll kick him out. So help me, I'll get rid of that hippie," I muttered under my breath.

It didn't take me long to learn his name—Tom Reynolds. Even as I pronounced it, I felt my teeth grit together. The first day that we had a discussion over some essays I had asked the students to study from one of their texts, I felt an even stronger revulsion toward him—almost one of threat.

"Throw out all the laws," he said. "We don't need 'em."

Several of the class attacked his arguments.

His repartee was instant. "Huh! Government! It's filled with graft. Do away with it," he shouted.

With vigor one classmate demanded logical support for his sweeping generalizations.

"Down with the establishment," he thundered.

Having angered most of the class he began to give specific examples to support his arguments. Oh, there were fallacies in his logic, but his arguments outwitted all but the sharpest students in the class.

At the end of the week I read the first set of essays from this class. Tom Reynolds' paper made me so angry that I grabbed my red-ink pen and began to scribble furiously. I criticized the logic. "You can poke holes in it," I wrote. I pointed out errors in sentence structure, in paragraph development, in punctuation. Having slashed every page with vitriolic comments, I began to cool down, then reread the paper. Repugnant as his statements were to me—threatening to my accepted beliefs—I discovered the force of some of his arguments, the originality of some ideas. At the bottom of the last page I commented on this, commended him for his vivid expressions.

When I handed back the essays I was aware of the smirk on his face as I gave him his paper. "Aha," the expression said, "made you mad, didn't I?"

From the side of my eye I watched his face as he scanned each page. He seemed puzzled by the comments at the end. I began to unbend toward him, but the sight of his dirty bare legs and feet, his unwashed body—his insolence, his defiance—could make the hair rise on the nape of my neck.

This undeclared war between Tom Reynolds and me continued for weeks. In class he gained a few followers who helped him "bait" me with their statements which were, I thought, threats to traditions, customs, and society in general. Iconoclasts, I called them in my mind.

Fortunately there were several literary gems in the text which led away from the fiery diatribe against the "hypocrisy of American way of life," as Tom called it. His appreciation of these writings was surprising, but sincere. His comments caused more peace in the classroom.

By the end of the semester he was stopping now and then when the class period was over to continue a discussion of some idea that he had found so intriguing that he felt we hadn't completed exploring its ramifications. A few times he came to my office, asked about other writings of these essay writers—of Thoreau and Emerson, of Aristotle and Socrates, of Marcus Aurelius.

I do not teach classes during the summer months. Sometimes I take courses at the university, but more often I travel with my husband or my children.

Once, during a particular summer, the dean of students asked me to come to the college for a meeting of the scholarship committee, of which I was a member. Going first to my office, I began to look at the accumulated stack of mail on my desk. With letter opener in hand I ripped open an envelope and began to read.

"Busy, Mrs. Townsend?" I heard and looked up to see the great bushy head of Tom Reynolds extended around the door casing. I was startled. I was sure that I was alone in the office section of the building. It was so completely quiet; I had expected to hear or see no one.

"Been missing you this summer," he said as he came in and sat in the chair by my desk. "Got time for a little gabbing?"

"Yes. I have a meeting after awhile. But as usual I came too early. What are you doing this summer?"

"Taking two literature courses—world literature, both

courses, the early and the modern. Having a great time reading. Never knew there was such brainy stuff written."

We discussed the authors he had been reading selections from.

"You're planning to be here in college this fall?"

"Nope! Got a job in Florida, working on fishing boats. I'll make a pile of money from tourists. Besides I've got to have time to sort out my thoughts. I'm not sure what I want to do with my life."

"I must leave to go to that meeting, but it's been good to talk with you," I said. "Maybe you'll come back to us next year."

Not once did I think of him during the following months. In October I found in my college mailbox a personal letter from him.

"Tom Reynolds, Tom Reynolds," I said aloud. "Who in the world is that?"

Even the Florida address gave me no clue. I tore open the envelope and began to read the letter, quickly snatching key phrases, "here on my job . . . nothing good to read . . . mind getting stagnant . . . wish I had something to challenge my thinking . . . send me some books . . . you choose them . . . be glad to pay you. . . ."

"Not really!" I said to the empty foyer where I stood, remembering distinctly this student who had been so revolutionary.

I went to my office and looked up at the shelves of books, many of them complimentary copies. I pulled out four—two anthologies, good collections that would be stimulating reading, a classic novel, and a book of modern short stories with provocative developments.

The next day I mailed these to Tom and later sent a short letter. I couldn't resist a visit to the dean's office to tell him of this conquest of my hippie's interest. Often this dean and I had sparred about traditional and modern, he jabbing at my clinging to the old customs, not accepting some of the modern.

"Evidently we 'traditional' teachers can still build rapport with the hippie," I said, bragging.

In December I had another letter from Tom Reynolds telling how eagerly he had been devouring the books I had sent. Near the end of his letter he said, "I'll be sending you something very soon. I hope you like it. I did it myself."

"Some writing he has done," I said to myself, pleased.

When the package came and I opened it, I had to take a second look at the sender's name and address. It couldn't be! But it was. Wrapped in layers of white paper was a small plaque made of dark wood, the surface shellacked and rubbed glossy. The edges of the plaque were purposely uneven, following the grooves of the wood grain. On the front had been painted two blue iris blossoms, Japanese iris, their lines perfectly drawn, their colors delicate in hue.

I stood looking at the gift, my mind struggling to relate this little work of art with the rough, wild appearance of my hippie student. Holding it, I walked to the office of another English teacher and explained my dilemma.

"You say it's from Tom Reynolds?" asked the other teacher.

"Yes, do you know him?"

"Had him in literature class this summer. That plaque is a real contrast to Tom."

I wrote to thank Tom for the gift, taking great care in my choice of words. One day at the end of the semester I came into my office, my arms filled with exam papers, and found Tom Reynolds waiting for me. My face must have registered my complete surprise.

"You remember me," he said, "don't you?"

"Yes, but give me a moment to think of your name."

"Just on vacation for a few days. Got to go back until the last of August. Then I'm quitting my job."

"What will you do then?"

"That's what I'm here preparing for now. I've been to the university getting transferred there, looking at the courses listed in that catalog, ones I can take this fall."

As we talked I observed Tom's appearance. He wore white pants, new and well-pressed, regular shoes, a blue shirt of silky-like cotton looking as if it had just come from the store. His long hair was combed neatly. Only the beard remained as his badge of youthful challenge to society, but even that was smooth, evenly trimmed.

"What do you plan to do with your education, Tom?" I asked.

"Well, you ought to know, Mrs. Townsend. I like to express my opinions. I want to write them some day. But in the meantime there is a lot of studying and reading that I want to do. Who knows?"

"Good enough!" I said. "I'll be looking for your articles. And when I see them I'll brag 'I knew him when he was a mere college freshman.' "

Giving and Receiving

Angela Benson was in my one o'clock class. That first afternoon, as I shuffled the orange registration cards and called the roll, she said, "Mrs." after I had pronounced her name. In the first week of gaining rapport with the class, listening carefully to the remarks of each student, thoughtfully reading each essay written, and observing the appearance of each class member, I categorized her—not much money, intensely sincere, purposeful, somewhat intimidated by fear of ridicule of her opinions. I learned that she was a mother and judged she was past thirty years old.

She was not a good student, but she learned rapidly, rewriting essays on which I had put red marks for mechanical errors. One Friday she did not attend class. On Monday she stopped at my desk as she entered the room.

"I had to take my little girl to the doctor for a tetanus shot," she explained simply. "But I have prepared the assignment. Will you accept it late?"

"Of course," I said.

She sat down, expelled a long-drawn-out breath—of weariness, I thought. I noticed her hands—rough, with broken nails. Her simple cotton dress was homemade, I was sure, not particularly stylish. Her hair was shining clean, but pulled back and fastened with a barrett at the nape of her neck.

The following week she turned in an essay that I had

assigned. It was a three-page theme of her reasons for returning to school at thirty-five. Her husband had developed a heart ailment. The doctors warned her that he could not work long at his job. There were three children, in grade and high school. She had taken part of their savings and entered our college, enrolling in a full load of classes, planning to become an elementary teacher by the time her husband had to retire completely because of his health.

My appreciation of her deepened as I learned more about her. She would be a competent teacher, I was confident. But could she manage her home, her studies, and find finances to pay for college tuition and fees?

At the next meeting of the scholarship committee, of which I was a member, I heard her name called by the secretary for the dean of student personnel.

"This Angela Benson has applied for a scholarship. Anyone know her, have her in class?"

"I do," I answered quickly. "She's a very good student."

The secretary glanced at her records. "I find that she lives just outside the limits of our community college district and therefore is ineligible for most of our scholarships. Besides, this means she must pay double the amount of money each semester that other students do."

"Let me tell you a little more about her problems," I offered and quickly related the details I had learned.

The dean lifted his head and tapped his pencil against his teeth.

"We can't help her, I'm afraid," he said thoughtfully. He shuffled the pages on which were listed the possible grants, loans, and scholarships. "Each scholarship is earmarked with certain stipulations. We are limited by these controls."

We turned our attention to other students on the list of applicants. As we were leaving I said, "This Mrs. Benson needs help. Let's see if we can scrounge around and find an organization or club that would be willing to finance a scholarship for her."

At the next meeting of this committee her name came up again. The secretary had investigated a bit and reiterated the facts of real need. But we found no solution.

All during the meeting I wriggled and twisted in my chair. At last I suggested "Why not have a Faculty Friends Scholarship and give the funds to Mrs. Benson? I can put in one hundred dollars!" During the quiet that followed I said to myself, "Soft heart, weak brain, darn it!"

A few of the faculty added to the amount.

"Let's make it anonymous," I went on. "Mrs. Benson is sensitive. We don't want this scholarship to smack of charity. She must not feel obligated to anyone. I have checked her grades in other classes. They're good. Besides," I added lamely, "I have her in my class. And I want her to hold her head high and feel she has earned a scholarship."

I wrote the check and passed it to the secretary.

One afternoon, about two weeks before the end of the first semester, Mrs. Benson stayed in her seat after the class was dismissed, waiting until all the students had streamed out of the room. Then she looked up at me. I saw the warm glow of happiness in her eyes.

"Mrs. Townsend, did you know that I have been given a scholarship that will pay for most of my registration fees for the next semester?"

Without waiting for my comments she hurried on, "My husband is so relieved, and I am just—oh—it has lifted my spirits. I was so worried. I did not want to take the last bit out of our savings. But I want to go on—I like college—I want to be a teacher—and isn't learning wonderful!"

I congratulated her and experienced with her the sense of

achievement, of acceptance, of honor earned. A few weeks later I found, clipped to her last essay, a short note.

"I received the money for the scholarship. The greater part was a check signed by you. Now, don't be disturbed that I know you are a donor. I am really pleased—so glad that you have confidence in me—that you care—that my teachers are interested in my college education. I want to live up to their expectations. I'll try."

For a few days I fretted over this error made by the secretary. Then I began to understand that it did not matter. Angela Benson was not embarrassed. I watched her as she continued to excel—in my next semester composition class, in my introduction to fiction class, in mythology and world literature. She gained knowledge, confidence, poise, and a sense of worth. Perhaps her knowing about the scholarship had given her security, as well as financial aid.

Loren Makes Me Proud

I had known the boy years before, when he was a senior in high school and he had come to my office for counseling.

"Loren, your tests show that you have great ability to learn and retain, yet you seem satisfied with mediocre grades. Why?"

"Oh, I have a good time!" he said and grinned unabashedly.

"I know you're a great center on the basketball team. You work hard at that."

"Yeah! Basketball is fun."

"But you plan to go to college?"

"Dunno."

"What do your parents think?"

"They want me to go, but I dunno."

"With grades such as you're making right now, you'll never be accepted by the best universities."

"Suits me," he said and flashed his infectious smile, his blue eyes clear and undisturbed.

I was teaching in college before I saw him again. He appeared at my home one evening.

"Mrs. Townsend, got time to talk awhile?" he said, debonair as ever.

"You know I have," I said as I beckoned him into the room.

For hours we sat at the dining room table, talking about college courses, about majors, minors, and various fields of study.

"I don't really want to go to college," he said as he left, "but I suppose I'll have a go at it to please Mom and Dad."

He called me at the end of the first semester. He was at home.

"You'll be unhappy to know that I flunked out. I have enlisted in the Navy. Maybe in four years I'll have a different attitude toward the whole thing. This is to say good-bye."

"Good luck, Loren," I answered. "Call me when you are home on leave if you have time." I sat looking at the telephone. Perhaps he will mature, I muttered to myself, learn something about himself, something about the world he lives in. . . .

Four years later I saw him again. He was out of the Navy, had come home from the Pacific. He dropped in to see me, looking older, talking seriously yet eagerly of his experiences in the Intelligence Unit of the Navy.

"I am fascinated by the Chinese people, their history, their politics, their antiquity, and their economy. I have been sent on many secret missions that have helped me learn much about them. Really, they've been a most unusual civilization. Always they have absorbed their conquerers. Give them time and they use the best ideologies of the people who take over their country and gradually discard the worst."

"What are you going to do now, Loren?" I was more interested in this fellow, personally, than in the Chinese.

"It sounds absurd," he said slowly. "My folks tried to talk me out of it, but I want to study Chinese culture. I want to go to the University of Hawaii. I have looked around at various colleges, but I like the department on Chinese there the best."

"A very good school, I've heard. I was on the campus when my husband and I were in Honolulu two years ago. I know one of the professors of the faculty. But it is very expensive. Can you swing it?"

"I want to try. I have saved a little money. Because of my four years of Navy service I have the GI Bill stipend. Also I have applied for a government student loan. I think I can make it."

"And you're ready to dig in and study?"

"I'm sure now. Will you write a letter of recommendation for me to this person?" He gave me a slip of paper with a name written on it.

"You bet. That's one of the joys of being a teacher."

In January I happened to meet Loren's father as I shopped in a hardware store.

"How's Loren?" I asked eagerly.

"He's had a great time at Hawaii University. And his letter this week reported that he had made the honor roll. That's a different Loren, isn't it?"

"He's found a reason for studying, I think."

"But the other part of his letter wasn't so good. The government loans to students have been cut severely right now. You probably have seen this in the papers. Well, being a new student, and an out-of-state student, he had his grant for next semester canceled. I'm so worried. You know I don't have money to give him—with one son in high school and two children in the grades, I haven't an extra cent. He wants to know whether he should give up and see if he can find a way to come home. He's tried to get work in Honolulu, but with the thousands of students concentrated there, that's impossible right now."

"How much money does he need to go this semester?"

"He has it figured out pretty closely—about a thousand

dollars. That's a lot of money; I can't raise it. Do you know any place he can turn to try to get a loan, a scholarship, a grant?"

"Not in Hawaii—no, nor here either, especially at mid-term as it is now. And it would be a shame to have him leave now that he's found his field."

We turned from the subject and talked of seeding the lawn, of weed controls, and then I left. When I got to the car where my son was waiting for me, I started the motor, then just sat with it idling for a moment. Abruptly I turned off the key and began to tell my son about Loren.

"Jim," I said, "you have some cash in the bank. Will you lend me five hundred dollars and I'll give it back after the first of the month?"

"Yes," he said.

I went back into the hardware store where I found Loren's father buying nails. As the clerk dropped the heavy metal pieces by handfuls onto the scoop of the scales, I talked to the father.

"I've decided to give you the money for Loren," I said. "I'll write a check out to him. You send it. Tell him I'm expecting great things from him."

As I busied myself writing the check, I looked away from the father. I was afraid he was going to cry. Then he cleared his throat and said huskily, "I wasn't asking for money from you, Mrs. Townsend. I had no idea—I just knew you would understand his problem—our problem—and I had to talk to someone."

"It's a good investment," I said.

About a month later the letter from Loren came. I saved it—it is precious to me. Also included in the envelope was a legal note made out to me for the full amount and signed by Loren.

Sometime in June his mother called me.

"I haven't tried to express my thanks before," she said. "I'd have sobbed like a baby. But you will want to hear this. Loren made the dean's list this semester. He wanted you to know. Besides that he has a good job at the airport now, works at night, says he can make it by himself now, even when college begins in the fall again."

For five years I just had scraps of information about him. Then in June, while hurrying down the hall in the hospital one day after visiting a friend, I was grabbed from behind and hugged affectionately. It was Loren's mother.

"Elsie, we've just had the news from Loren. He finished his master's degree at the university and has flown directly to Washington, D.C. He has been accepted for a position in the State Department because of his knowledge of Chinese politics and culture, and because of his college record and his work in Navy Intelligence in the Pacific. I was going to call you."

We did a few dance steps there in the hall in the hospital in sheer exultation. Nurses stopped and stared, but we were oblivious of their wonder. We were in another world—a world where dreams come true, where a young man responds to a stimulus and achieves success through hard work and perseverance.

"And a special message for you," she said. "Loren said as soon as he got his finances caught up a bit, he was going to begin to pay you back. Your name is top on his list, he said."

"That's not the important thing," I objected, returning to the mundane existence of dollars and cents. "What is paramount is that he fulfilled our hopes in him. He achieved his first goal. Now for the future—tell him how proud of him I am."

"You know I will!"

Faith in Mankind

The class began as usual. I picked up the packet of peach-colored IBM cards, pulled off the rubber band, held the packet up to the light to see that the holes matched.

"I'm looking to see whether I have a student in here who is not registered for this course," I explained to the class.

I put on my glasses and said, "I'll try to pronounce your names. If I make a mistake, tell me. You've had them ever since you were born. It's the first time I've seen them. If you're a Mrs. instead of a Miss, and want that title, please tell me."

I paused and looked up. There were just bored expressions on their faces.

"Emil Adams?"

"Yeah."

"Frank Atkins."

"Accounted for here."

I went on down to the bottom of the stack of cards. A small class for World Literature II, I thought. Good opportunity for discussion! I noticed two housewives—women in their mid-thirties—one fellow twenty-five or thirty or so, the others just from high school.

The air was hot and humid; the students were sweaty and uncomfortable. Now and then they moved their bodies to keep from sticking to the seats. I mopped my face, taking off all makeup ruthlessly. I passed out assignment sheets and began to lecture on the purpose of the course and the historical background of the period we would begin to study.

At the end of the period the students walked out of the room passively, not even speaking to each other, apparently not acquainted at all.

During the next session, we talked of Pascal, his wager, his "Pensees."

"What a dumb guy," one student commented. "Off the deep end on religion."

"He might have made some real contributions if he'd stayed with his calculus," another said. They scoffed at Pascal's wager.

Later, with *Samson Agonistes* I had like responses.

"Nobody—like nobody—could be so superstitious as to believe that he had been given a special mission on earth. This business of an angel talking to his father—nonsense! Who's ever seen an angel?"

I looked at the speaker. His voice was almost a sneer. Checking my seating chart I found his name—Steve Hearn.

Two women—the married ones—attempted to defend the religious concepts of the epic, but the other students joined the first speaker in attacks on idealism, religion, the idea of being created for a purpose.

"Strength in his hair! Ha!" one said and several laughed. The younger girls in the class followed the pattern of the fellows.

"But he had taken an oath—a vow," defended one of the married women.

As we read one selection after another, Steve Hearn led the class in ridicule of any idealism, any romance, any religious sincerity. He was quick with his arguments, mentally acute; he slashed away at any sentiment or altruistic emotion.

241

He would wait until the class had mauled over the plot and the motives of the characters and then shoot his hand up into the air. With my nod he would begin his tirade against "hypocrites" and "whited sepulchers."

"People are all that way," he'd say. "I know. Don't trust 'em. They're such liars, two-faced. I've been working for ten years as a reporter for the newspaper. I've met all kinds—mayors, governors, big businessmen, politicians, even Scout leaders. They say one thing—live another."

His bitter cynicism carried through the class.

Tartuffe he relished. "Now that's a real story," he said and he commented on the realism of the two protagonists. "Hypocrites, these churchmen. Same old sixes and sevens. Out for a quick buck."

With the exception of the two older women, the class agreed with him. When we read Gide, Steve was delighted. He came to my office before class.

"I read *Theseus*—almost all of it before I caught on. It's really an autobiography of the author, isn't it, not really a story of the mythological character. Sensual old fool, wasn't he? But an accurate picture of men today!"

"The Greek story of Theseus," I began, but he interrupted me.

"Just man, as sensual as ever," he said quickly.

We talked for an hour or more. He laughed at my "rose-colored glasses" philosophy, my idealism, but not so harshly as he had at the beginning of the semester.

The obscenity, the earthiness, of the *Caucasian Chalk Circle* delighted the younger students of the class.

"Here's real life," they said. "People talk this way." They relished the four-letter words of the dialogue and laughed at the crudeness of the judge. Steve was unusually quiet during the class discussion of this play. We attended a performance of the play on the stage at the university—fortunately appearing at that time.

On the last day of the semester we were considering *No Exit.*

One of the married women protested the existentialism of the play. "Makes life seem so empty and bare and purposeless," she said.

"I just don't buy it," the other older woman said.

Steve was interested in the perfection of the plot development, the clever balance of characters, the ecstasy of emotional torture suggested. Halfway through the class period he suddenly threw his pencil onto his desk with a sharp crack, rested his elbows on the tabletop, and said slowly, "Mrs. Townsend, all the way through this course you've said repeatedly, 'This is what the author is saying' or 'A certain literary critic makes this observation.' But often I've been aware that you did not agree with the sentiment of the writer, particularly the surrealistic ones. I am sure you do not accept Sartre's idealogy of existentialism. Now—what do you believe? Do you believe in—say—creation?"

I caught my breath and stood looking at the students. Their heads were lifted, their faces expectant. But there was no scorn on their lips, no smug expressions denoting, "Well, now for some old-fashioned platitudes from the establishment!"

Rapidly the thoughts raced through my head. A teacher is forbidden to teach religion in tax-supported schools—state law! How foolish. Teachers could force on students ideas of atheism, of agnosticism, of deism—oh, that's okay. But religion—hands off!

I lifted my head and said to myself, "The administration can fire me. I can lose my job. But I'm going to answer this young man. I must."

"Yes, Steve," I said firmly, my heart pounding so hard that my chest felt crowded. "I do believe in creation; I believe in a great Creator."

I waited a moment. There was no sound in the room. The students still looked up at me, and their eyes were not scornful.

"I know there is a purpose in creation," I continued. "There is a reason for my being here and for each one of you. And I believe that this life is not the end. I must prepare for more than this, the life after this one."

I stopped, prepared for an outburst. No one stirred. Every eye was fixed on mine. But I read no distrust, no ridicule. Quickly I returned to the class discussion of the play before us, and then we went on to talk of Faulkner's story in their text.

After class was dismissed I fumbled with my lecture notes, my hands still trembling, my mind wandering. The following week the class met for final examination. As each student finished and brought his papers to me, I talked in low voice to him or her, usually about his next semester plans. The two hours had passed before Steve brought his pages of fine writing to my desk. I walked with him to the classroom door. He started to go, then turned to face me.

"Mrs. Townsend," he said quietly, "I want you to know this. For years now, I have had no faith in mankind, no hope. You've given me back these two things. I feel I must thank you for this."

He went on through the door and I went back to my desk.

The last student in the room—one of the housewives—came to me with her last papers.

"What will you be taking next semester?" I asked.

"I won't be in college," she said.

"You've enjoyed the class, haven't you?"

"You know I have. It has given me a peek at a whole new world. But my son needs the car so he can attend the university. Besides my husband says it's foolish to spend money to pour facts into the head of a woman who is merely a housewife."

"Oh, no! I think it is very important for each person to learn, for the mind to develop, to acquire knowledge, gain concepts."

She stood a moment, gaining control of her emotions.

"He says, 'Why?' I'm not important, he says, and studying literature won't make me a better cook or dish-washer."

"Everyone's important. You're a person, aren't you? And you influence many other people. You're a citizen. And you make this country a better place for us to live in by your thinking and your actions. You're a mother and a wife. What you think and know enriches your life and that of your home."

She looked up at me and smiled.

"Sounds good to me," she said. "But I'm afraid I can't convince my family."

We walked out into the hall and found Steve waiting there. He came close.

"Did I hear you say you needed a ride to college next semester?" he asked. "In what part of the city do you live?"

She gave her address and described the area of the town.

"Give me a few days and I'll bet I can get a ride for you. I'll find someone who lives near you who is attending Junior College. Give me your telephone number."

I left them there talking, my heart warm and glowing.

When the second semester began I wondered about this housewife. I watched for her in the halls. One day I saw her friend, the other married woman of that last semester's class. I questioned her.

"Do you know whether Mrs. Brennen is taking classes this semester?"

"Yes. I see her almost every day. She's in my psychology class—taking a history course too, I think."

"How does she get here to college?"

"She rides with some student down in her part of the city. He won't take any pay; says he has to go right by her door anyway."

We hurried on our way to classes.

In my office the next day I was bent over a pile of English essays, red-ink pen poised above them, when I heard someone at the open doorway.

"Hello, Mrs. Townsend."

"Steve! How nice! How are you doing this semester?"

We chatted awhile, then he said urgently, "Mrs. Townsend, do you know whether Mrs. Brennen is coming to college this semester?"

"That I do! I talked to her friend yesterday. Thanks, Steve!"